The Whole Story

The Whole Story

Crafting Fiction in the Upper Elementary Grades

Karen Jorgensen

HEINEMANN
Portsmouth, New Hampshire

Heinemann
A subsidiary of Reed Elsevier Inc.
361 Hanover Street
Portsmouth, NH 03801–3912
www.heinemann.com

Offices and agents throughout the world

Library of Congress Cataloging-in-Publication Data
Jorgensen, Karen L.
    The whole story : crafting fiction in the upper elementary grades /
Karen Jorgensen.
      p. cm.
    Includes bibliographical references.
    ISBN 0-325-00292-4 (pbk.)
    1. Creative writing (Elementary education).   2. Fiction—Study and teaching
(Elementary). I. Title.

    LB1576. J67 2001
    372.62'3—dc21   00-054091

Editor: William Varner
Production: Vicki Kasabian
Cover design: Joni Doherty
Manufacturing: Deanna Richardson

Printed in the United States of America on acid-free paper

04   03   02   01   00   RRD   1   2   3   4   5

To my daughter, Gita Esmaili, a writer whose insights into the soul and passion for words taught me the profound power of the story.

Contents

Acknowledgments

I began *The Whole Story* seven years ago in Kira Walker's fifth-grade classroom at Washington School. I was the Title I teacher then, working with a group of Kira's struggling readers and writers. For two years we investigated how these youngsters used their sense of place to generate story ideas and create settings. I brought this experience with me when I entered my own classroom as a fifth-grade teacher several years later. I am indebted to Kira not only for her contributions to this early research but also for her honest, insightful, and often humorous comments on multiple drafts of this book.

I also am grateful to James Venable, another colleague at Washington, who, over the years, has patiently listened to my ramblings and musings as I struggled to find my voice in *History Workshop* and now, in this piece. James is an experienced writing teacher, a colleague whose comments repeatedly caused me to rethink the substance and presentation of this project. I also want to thank Karen Toloui for her advice and support during the past year and a half. Karen suggested resources and read the manuscript several times, posing questions from her unique perspective as a college writing teacher. Finally, I wish to acknowledge Bill Varner, my editor at Heinemann. Bill's critical yet encouraging comments helped bring this book to publication.

Of course, there wouldn't be a book without my students, scores of young writers like Lori and Ronnie, Susan and Steven, whose delightful spirit and energy inspired this undertaking from the very beginning.

The Whole Story

Introduction

When animal droppings and garbage and spoiled straw are piled up in a great heap, the rotting and moiling give forth heat. Usually no one gets close enough to notice because of the stench. But the girl noticed and, on that frosty night, burrowed deep into the warm, rotting muck, heedless of the smell. In any event, the dung heap probably smelled little worse than everything else in her life—the food scraps scavenged from kitchen yards, the stables and sties she slept in when she could, and her own unwashed, unnourished, unloved, and unlovely body. (Cushman 1995, 1)

Revulsion best describes my feelings when I read the lead to Karen Cushman's *The Midwife's Apprentice* (1995). But Alyce's struggle to survive as a twelve-year-old orphan in rural fourteenth-century England pulled me into the story by the end of the first chapter. I read it in one evening, reluctant to leave this young girl's side as she navigates her way through a taunting circle of teasing village boys, a demeaning job scouring tables with river sand at the local inn, and the cruel insults of the village midwife who discovers her in the dung heap. Cushman creates an intelligent, passionate, complex character whose inherent dignity and tenacious will to survive moves the story along.

Like other memorable fiction, *The Midwife's Apprentice* is more than plot, more than setting. It's driven by characters we remember long after we close the book, characters who mirror our worries, desires, and determination, who reflect our sense of compassion and our joy. On some level, children understand this, too, but remain media addicts used to high-impact action, quick scene changes, and characters who flash by without leaving a trace—no connections, no memories, not much to ponder. They bring this sense of story to the writers' workshop, where I, as a teacher, often feel as if I'm in the rehab business, trying to help authors resee the world and discover the potential stories that quietly lie in the hearts and minds of the characters these youngsters create. It's not an easy task, but I believe that ten-year-olds possess the requisite tools to do this. It's my job to help them find the whole story and tell it well.

As always, I begin with the intentions and experiences of my students, balancing those with what I believe are the hallmarks of well-crafted fiction. Sometimes this means stretching writers beyond what they know, beyond their growing knowledge of the world, beyond their youthful understanding of the way we tell stories. I teach craft, yet I respect the imaginary worlds they create, worlds based on experience, filtered through feelings and the scrim of memory. Fiction is an abstraction, once removed from experience, an extrapolation of reality that invites ten-year-olds to experiment and role play. I think this is why they love it so much and why it's so difficult to teach.

Teaching fiction is especially challenging in the west end of Alameda, California, where I've been a resource and classroom teacher for the past thirteen years. My students' parents sometimes work two jobs and don't always supervise homework or read bedtime stories. Many kids speak one language at home and another at school. It's a stable community, though; most children spend kindergarten through eighth grade at Washington School. This book is a response to these learners and somewhat of a departure from the orthodoxies I've grown to associate with "writers' workshop." Short, suggestive interventions, the five-minute conferences and lessons I used with questionable success for so many years, don't work with these students. My talks are longer now, my teaching more direct. These writers need lots of time to think through ideas, so I give well-paced lessons, not minilessons, and some of them last for days. We revisit concepts over and over again, allowing students plenty of time to learn from peers and to practice new techniques. I also directly teach, not suggest, ways to write fiction, exposing students to a series of strategies I believe will help them craft better stories.

I base these strategies on a blend of inquiry and modeling. *Inquiry*, the inductive process of gathering and interpreting information, encourages construction of abstractions from concrete, firsthand experience. We practice inquiry as writers by observing daily experience and using this insight to develop characters, setting, and plot. I borrow this approach from history, science, and mathematics, where we interpret primary sources, conduct experiments, or manipulate tangrams and unifex cubes before exploring historical causation, evaluating scientific theories, or solving algorithms.

Modeling, the act of demonstrating a skill or thought process, shows students how skilled authors go about the craft of storytelling. After demonstrations I invite students to imitate the master artist. These approaches complement each other: inquiry provides the raw material of fiction, the information about the world that authors use to create people, places, and plot. Modeling introduces ways to construct text, to turn experience into written story.

I use conferences to individualize lessons, tailoring what we learn in whole group to the needs of writers working on particular pieces. I frustrate writers if I'm too obtuse in these conferences, if I leave them with a series of questions and no advice, so I've learned to give honest opinions, offer suggestions, and model—if not compose—leads, scenes, or dialogue. I've come to believe that this is the only way many students internalize the subtle complexities of telling a good story.

This experience has led me to rethink the function of peer shares, teacher conferences, and lessons. I used to believe that writers learn as much about storytelling from peers as they do from me. I don't think that's true anymore. Shares are essential to the writing process. They are irreplaceable ways to generate story ideas, encourage risk taking, build a sense of audience, and set the tone for the workshop; but ten-year-olds learn the craft of writing primarily from me, through carefully planned lessons and interactive conferences. I am a stronger mentor now because I realize that I know more about the storytelling craft than the youngsters I teach. This new balance, this subtle shift from peer to student–teacher interaction, offers a structured way to teach writing without losing the spirit of a child-centered curriculum. It also moves the workshop in a new direction, one that places greater emphasis on the expertise, experience, and wisdom of the adult learner, the classroom teacher.

The writing samples, drawings, and dialogues in this book represent a cross section of learners, though most examples come from my 1998–1999 fourth–fifth multiage classroom. I tape-recorded almost all my conferences and lessons with these students and saved original artwork and stories. When I selected work for the manuscript, I tried to select from a range of students—from mature and reflective ones like Lori and Steven, to younger, less-developed writers like Ronnie and Olivia. I wanted to show a variety of responses, to give a clear, authentic view of teaching fiction to ten-year-olds in settings similar to Washington School.

In some ways *The Whole Story* is genre-specific—addressing the complex act of telling a good story—but it's also a book about writing, about becoming aware of experience, of sensing sights, sounds, and smells, of dipping into what writers know to extrapolate, to construct, to imagine, and to describe. For me, it's an unfinished work. Every year I begin again, watching and rethinking. Should I start with scenes this year or begin by teaching students how to observe the world as writers? Does it matter which way I start? Is this group too shy to perform skits, too rowdy to take a story trip, too unfocused to gather information on the playground? How can I adapt activities to meet the needs of this new class? The questions never stop, and what I do one year usually changes the next. I've captured a moment in time in these pages, all the while remembering that teaching is a dynamic, ongoing process, a restless adventure with no right answers, no clear solutions.

FICTION AND THE YOUNG WRITER

I've learned about the intentions and experiences of young writers by watching, listening, and questioning as they interact with one another and with me. In these moments I confirm previous thoughts, confront new puzzles, and arrive at deeper insights. I recall an afternoon a couple of years ago when I was in the middle of a conference with Jessica, a fifth-grader in our classroom at Washington School. We were discussing revisions she'd made to her piece about a young girl who finds a magic shell on the beach. In the middle of our conversation the working hum of writing voices turned into a louder, less-focused mixture of play and discussions about lunch menus, who likes whom, and kickball teams. As I scanned the room I saw Mustafa, Jacob, and Steven hunched over Paulo's collection of Wolverine cards, and Susan and Lori giggling on the floor while five or six other writers were busy laughing, talking, and roaming about the room. I stopped the workshop and brought them together into a writers' circle to discuss balancing talk, play, and story construction. I asked why they liked writing fiction. We waited a few moments before Judy said she "can make up stories from [her] head." Susan agreed, adding that her stories were more interesting than her "boring life." Paulo commented that he wanted to write stories this year because he doesn't like essays, and "that's all you get to do in sixth grade." Several students nodded. When Jessica's turn came, she said she liked the workshop because she can "get [her] feelings out." Others said that they enjoyed sharing their stories with writers in the room. Ricky, James, and Patrick concurred, adding that "the best part is making [stories] up with other kids." We went on to discuss the purposes of our sharing time and ended our circle with a joint commitment to work more productively the next day.

I remember this discussion for several reasons. It refocused our energy, but it also revealed how much young writers value fiction. I wasn't surprised. I know children love fiction. I observe it in our classroom, and I'd seen it for years when I worked as a resource teacher at Washington. Children love to hear it, read it, think about it, talk about it, illustrate it, construct it quietly or in animated groups. They write stories in kindergarten, and by fifth grade, fiction becomes a passion. By ten, children truly discover that, as Kieran Egan (1988, 96–97) says, "We are a storying animal; we make sense of things commonly in story form; ours is a largely story-shaped world."

For a long time I wondered what to do with this passion. Every time I thought about teaching fiction to ten-year-olds, another image came to mind. I pictured myself sitting at the dining room table with a stack of writing folders, shaking my head, feeling completely frustrated and overwhelmed. By adult standards, most fifth-graders write terrible fiction: placeless settings; illogical, derivative plots; stereotypical, motiveless characters. It took me a while to figure out why kids do this. Here's what I've observed: In their stories, kids use characters from movies, TV, and video games or characters based on classmates and family—all personae they assume the audience knows. Thus, ten-year-olds don't feel a need to show how these actors think, talk, or move. It's really the *action* that counts. After all, that's what kids see in the mass media. Story plots resemble TV commercials in which one action quickly follows the next. Sometimes there's a climax but not always. All events in these shapeless stories seem equally important, and although the action invites *showing,* writers usually tell it, leaving us wondering what never makes it to the page. Mustafa's "Gary and Matt" is typical fifth-grade fiction:

> On a cold and windy night Matt the rat tried to sneak food in his rat hole, but Gary the cat wants to eat Matt. Gary tries and tries, but he can't catch him. He tries every day but he can't get him. He tries everything in the "Meet the Rat, Eat the Rat" book, all 1,556 books. Gary blew up the house two times and stuck fifty dynamites in Matt's rat hole. He even put a thousand rat traps in the house, but Gary fell over and got all the traps stuck on him.

Mustafa tells the story and doesn't show the fat rat he develops by the fourth draft. He summarizes the action, unaware that he could show how "Gary tries and tries but he can't catch him" through dramatic movement and dialogue.

I turned to Donald Graves' *Experiments with Fiction* (1989) looking for ways to improve these stories. I also read about fiction in the writing books I often consulted for inspiration and advice.[1] These resources were useful, but I needed more. I wasn't looking for a sequence of prescriptive lessons but rather an approach to the day-to-day construction of stories with young writers. I wanted to know where to begin and how to proceed. I needed to hear teachers and students in dialogue, discussing characterization, setting, plot, and theme. I finally turned to books for adult writers. Here I discovered how mature storytellers learn to craft characters, to develop scenes, to select point of view, and to shape a piece. Questions formed as I read: What characterizes good fiction? Why do kids like to write it? What's difficult for them? Why should I teach it? How should I teach it? I addressed these questions during the last few years and, in trying out new ideas, developed a process for teaching fiction writing to fifth-graders; but I use the word *process* with reservations. This book doesn't contain a formula but presents a chronicle of my observations, a summation of my thoughts over the past five years. I modify the way I teach story writing each year as I learn about my students, molding *the process* to meet their unique interests and needs.

So what makes a good piece of fiction? There's no right answer to this question, but we know when a story pleases us, moves us, makes us laugh, scares us. We identify with powerful stories because they teach us something about ourselves. As James Gardiner (1984) suggests, "The primary subject of fiction is and has always been human emotion, values, and beliefs" (14–15). Good stories are character-driven, and the writer's business is to "make up convincing human beings and create for them basic situations and actions by means of which they come to know themselves and reveal themselves to the reader." The writer's authority, then, is grounded "partly in his . . . ability to perceive and understand the world around him and partly in his experience as a craftsman" (9). The writer brings his or her experience to the story and learns the craft of telling it through study, imitation, and practice.

Like mature authors, fifth-graders possess the requisite experience and emotional tools to craft fictional worlds with authority and authenticity. They know what it is to be sad or lonely, to feel confused, curious, or scared. They've fought with brothers and sisters, laughed at funny jokes, cried over a lost pet, and felt the mixture of fear and excitement that accompanies breaking adult rules or riding a high-speed roller coaster. They vicariously experience people's lives through TV, movies, and video games. The writing teacher's job is to tap into this reservoir of feelings, this repertoire of experience, to give it a name, and to show young authors how to incorporate the things they know into their work. It's a twofold task: helping writers discover the story and teaching them how to tell it well. Therein lies the crux of the problem and the central focus of this book: what do we do to move writers from action-driven narrative to stories about people, stories that "make [readers] see and feel vividly what [the] characters see and feel?" (Gardiner 1984, 43). How do we guide students to use what they know about the world to discover the whole story?

I start with the assumption that fiction is a craft that "like the carpenter's tricks, can be studied and taught" (Gardiner 1984, 7–8). I've learned that young authors need repeated exposure to good writing, and lots of practice. They also need to try out fiction techniques in whole-class exercises and then be shown, in demonstration lessons and in conferences, how to transfer these isolated skills to daily writing. I begin this yearlong process, this refocusing of narrative on characters, by teaching students how to write scenes, vivid character-centered sections of stories. We perform skits, take story trips, and develop scenes in daily writing. Then I lead students through a series of lessons designed to explore the details of characterization. I teach them to observe like writers, to note how people look, to watch how they move, to listen to what they say, and to wonder what all these observations reveal about attitudes and motives. All the while, we practice the craft of storytelling by rewriting characters and refining plot and setting.

I teach fiction writing as much as I can, balancing it with other genres and the constraints imposed by state and local curriculum. I tell parents at Back to School Night what I've observed: as children learn to write better fiction they acquire a deep understanding of stories. They develop *fiction sense* as they craft a scene, write an opening sentence, develop action, create a character, and recognize these elements in the books they read. They also learn to think clearly while clarifying plot and organizing ideas. As they discover these story elements they see that fiction, like all writing, reflects and re-creates experience. In their passion to construct make-believe worlds, they expand their sense of audience and develop fluency, seeing themselves as thinkers and as writers. This is demanding, rigorous work: fiction is the medium; reading, writing, and thinking are the goals.

Like others, I've observed that children write fiction early, developing elaborate pieces by second grade.[2] Some come to it gradually, fictionalizing personal narrative as a transition into the world of made-up stories. These writers add fiction to personal stories to create humor or heighten drama. I asked students about this not too long ago. Jacob said that he "adds stuff to make it more interesting." Patrick commented that "without the part where the dog bleeds [in "Thor"] it was going to be real boring." Olivia said that she fictionalized her camping piece "just to change it a little so kids will like it." Tommy added to his story about sledding because "the first time I wrote it, it was only half a page. There was this big jump, all of a sudden I was racing and then I scrubbed. I decided to put some talking in there because it was too short and pretty confusing." And Beth shared that

Chronology of Issues and Interventions

	What Good Writers Know	*Ways to Explore What Good Writers Know*
Moving Toward Character-Driven Narrative	Characters drive stories.	*Performing Skits.* Students act out two-minute impromptu plays showing two characters solving a problem.
	Characters interact in specific places.	*Taking Story Trips.* The class takes a series of walks to gather information and write scenes. Students practice again at home.

	Scenes show characters interacting.	*Developing Scenes in Daily Writing*
		1. The group spends several workshops selecting, drawing, sharing, and rewriting scenes from stories-in-progress.
		2. The teacher demonstrates scene writing.
		3. Writers discuss scenes in ongoing peer shares and student-teacher conferences. Respondents ask questions like:
		   "What makes this a scene?"
		   "Why is this a good place in the story for a scene?"
		   "What do you think about this scene?"
		   "How do the characters feel about each other in this scene?"
		   "How do you show how they feel?"
		   "What do we learn about the characters in this scene?"
		   "What could you add to make this scene better?"

Observing Like a Writer	Characters are people who look unique and dress differently.	*Observing Appearance* 1. Writers observe and discuss the unique appearance of classroom peers. 2. Writers observe the unique appearance of relatives, friends, and neighbors at home.
	Characters are people who move.	*Watching Movement* 1. Writers watch peers move on the playground at recess. 2. Writers watch the movement of relatives, friends, and neighbors at home.
	Characters are people who hesitate, interrupt, and gesture when they talk.	*Listening to How People Talk* 1. Writers listen to peers talk at lunchtime in the cafeteria. 2. Writers listen to relatives, friends, and neighbors talk at home.

FIG. I–1: A Writing Year

Characters are people whose movements and talking reveal feelings.

Writers show appearance.

Writers create meaningful dialogue.

Writers show movement.

Writers use movement and dialogue to reveal feelings.

Writers use mental landscapes to create settings.

Writers gather information to picture unfamiliar settings.

Writers discover plot.

Writers construct logical plots.

Writers create a focus or "conflict" in the plot.

Stories have meaning.

Writing with a Partner

1. Partners write actions to show feelings.
2. Partners write quotations to show feelings.

Rewriting Characters, Setting, and Plot

1. Writers learn more about character presentation, showing setting, and clarifying plot through lessons:
   a. Slipping appearance details into the story.
   b. Balancing dialogue and action.
   c. Writing dialogue and action to show feelings.
   d. Remembering what you know about places.
   e. Seeing out of the character's eyes.
   f. Charting plot "jumps."
   g. Learning "lessons" from characters.

2. Writers apply lessons in peer shares and student-teacher conferences. Respondents ask questions like:
   "How do you show how your character looks?"
   "Does your story contain too much dialogue?"
   "How's the character feeling when she says that?"
   "How can you describe what your character's doing?"
   "How's your character feeling when he does that?"
   "What could she do to show us how she feels?"
   "What could she say to show us how she feels?"
   "Where does the action take place?"
   "Do you picture this place?"
   "Have you ever been to a place like this? Tell me about it."
   "What can you add to help us picture it better?"
   "What's the story problem?"
   "What happens next?"
   "What can we learn from your story?"

FIG. I–1: *Continued*

she "made up that part about the people yelling because I wanted to make something funny."

Many fifth-graders begin the workshop writing personal narrative, then often switch to fiction by midyear. The mix and frequency of genres in these stories varies from classroom to classroom and from one year to the next. I see a lot of realism and fantasy. "Lip Gloss" is typical fifth-grade realism. Sandy's story takes place in a classroom. Her characters, modeled after two of her friends, dislike each other and spend the bulk of writers' workshop engaged in put-downs and insults. In Mustafa's fantasy "Garry and Matt," Matt's a fat, hungry mouse, Garry's a predatory cat. After an unsuccessful attempt to steal cheese from the table, Matt scurries back to his hole and mutters, "Man, that was close." Like many fantasies, "Garry and Matt" is based on a TV cartoon.

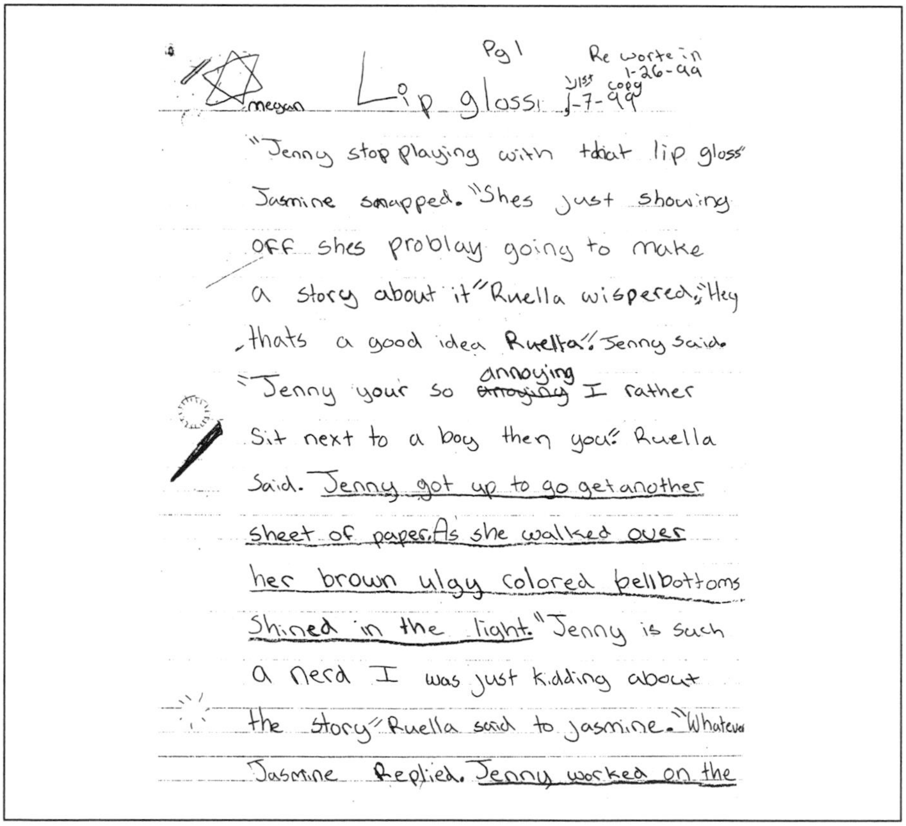
Pg 1
Re worte in 1-26-99
copy
megan Lip gloss 1-7-99
"Jenny stop playing with that lip gloss"
Jasmine snapped. "Shes just showing
off shes problay going to make
a story about it" Ruella wispered. "Hey
thats a good idea Ruella" Jenny said.
"Jenny your so annoying I rather
Sit next to a boy then you" Ruella
Said. Jenny got up to go get another
sheet of paper. As she walked over
her brown ulgy colored bellbottoms
Shined in the light. "Jenny is such
a nerd I was just kidding about
the story" Ruella said to jasmine. "Whatever"
Jasmine Replied. Jenny worked on the

FIG. I–2: "Lip Gloss": Fifth-grade Realism

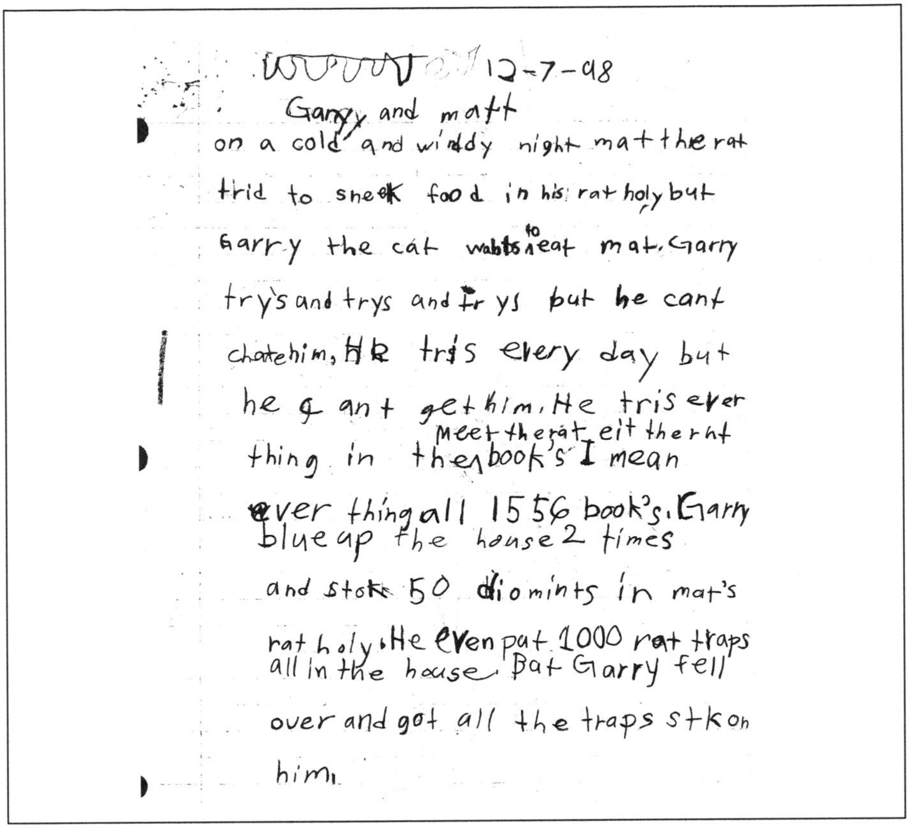

12-7-98
Garry and matt
on a cold and widdy night mat the rat
trid to sneek food in his rat holy but
Garry the cat wabts to eat mat. Garry
try's and trys and trys but he cant
chatch him, He trys every day but
he cant get him. He tris ever
thing in the [meet the rat eit the rat] book's I mean
ever thing all 1556 book's. Garry
blue up the house 2 times
and stole 50 diomints in mat's
rat holy. He even pat 1000 rat traps
all in the house. Bat Garry fell
over and got all the traps stk on
him.

FIG. I–3: "Garry and Matt": Fifth-grade Fantasy

Every year I also see a smattering of science fiction and mystery. Horror stories are always popular, especially among the boys. Sometimes these stories are realistic, like Patrick and Jacob's collaboration "Keep It Unlocked." In this piece, Patrick and Jacob play the characters. During a sleepover at Patrick's house, his parents leave, a storm disrupts the power, and an intruder stalks them while they're downstairs rummaging through the refrigerator for a snack. Tony's "Camp Horror" contains elements of fantasy. Five boys win tickets to a camp and spend the day hiding from a bloodthirsty monster. Tony attempts to create suspense with ghoulish characters and surprising plot twists, adapting ideas from several of R. L. Stine's (1995, 1996, 1998) summer camp stories.

Fifth-graders borrow heavily from books, films, TV, and video games. Surrounded by media images, they select and adapt ideas from sitcoms,

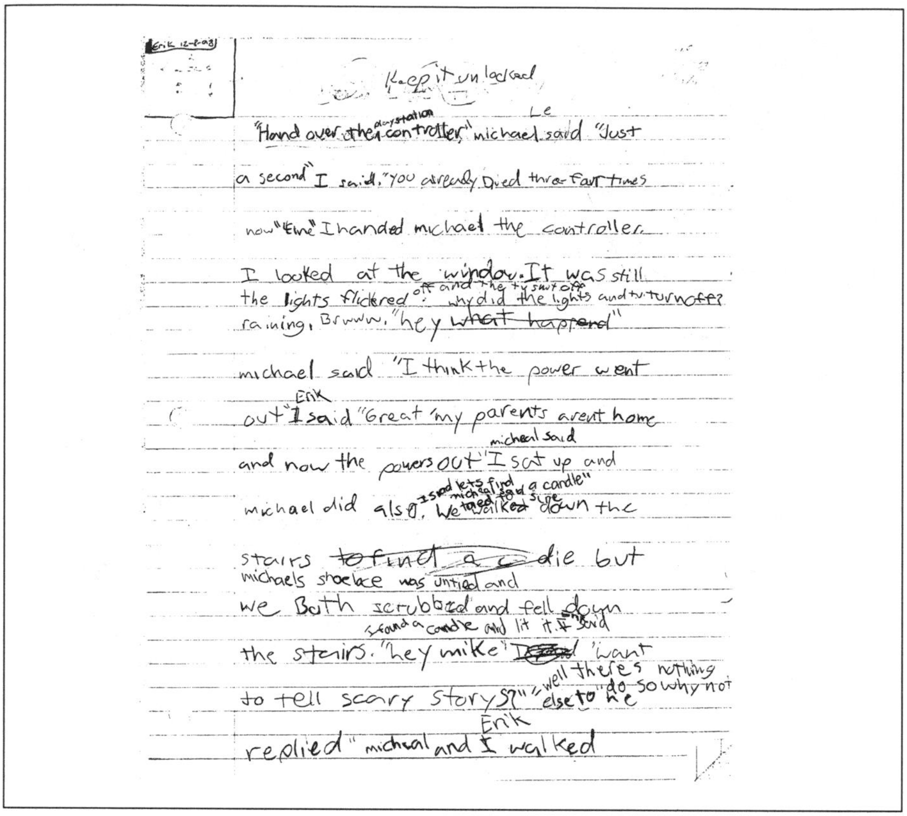
Erik 12-8-03

Keep it unlocked

"Hand over the playstation controller," michael said "Just a second" I said, "You already Died three four times now" "Fine" I handed michael the controller.

I looked at the window. It was still raining, Brwww. the lights flickered off and the tv shut off "why did the lights and tv turn off?" "hey what happend"

michael said "I think the power went out" Erik said "Great my parents arent home and now the powers out" michael said I sat up and michael did also. I said lets find a candle" michael said sure We walked down the stairs to find a candle but michaels shoelace was untied and we Both scrubbled and fell down the stairs. I found a candle and lit it. I said "hey mike" want to tell scary storys?" "well theres nothing else to do so why not" he replied" michael and Erik walked

FIG. I–4: "Keep It Unlocked": Fifth-grade Horror

PlayStation, *Goosebumps,* and popular movies. In these "playful appropriations" writers retell scenes from shows and dot fictional landscapes with superheroes (Dyson 1997, 7). These drafts hold wonderful potential, the raw material for original, well-constructed fiction; however, to turn first attempts into whole stories, writers need organized workshops where teachers model ways to talk about fiction and encourage the critical examination of ideas. In the next section I describe how I organize time and resources, addressing the everyday physical requirements and operational procedures necessary to carry on a workshop. I also show how I guide conversation to support young fiction writers, introducing lessons, conferences, and shares, which are discussed in detail throughout the remainder of the book.

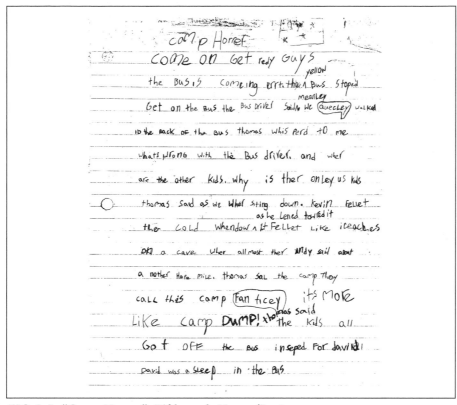

FIG. I–5: "Camp Horror": Fifth-grade Horror/Fantasy

NOTES

1. See sections on fiction writing in Calkins (1989, 1991), Graves (1994), and Atwell (1998).

2. *Contemporary Childhood, Popular Culture, and Classroom Literacy* (1997).

1

The Fiction Workshop

ORGANIZING THE CLASSROOM

Writers' workshop requires a predictable, well-organized setting where young authors can feel free to take risks. Room arrangements, time, writing materials, methods to ask for shares and conferences, clear behavioral standards, predictability—these elements make the workshop possible. A well-organized classroom promotes the continual flow of story ideas.

Lucy Calkins (1989, 1991), Nanci Atwell (1998), and others (Harste, Short, and Burke 1988; Graves 1994) have written volumes on how to organize a writers' workshop. Over the years I've used or modified their ideas, borrowed others from colleagues, and made up procedures of my own. I try things out; if they don't work, I rethink and try again. Our workshop is an eclectic mix that works for my students and for me.

I set aside over an hour and a half every day for writing. We usually begin with a thirty-minute quiet write. During this time students work silently while I conduct conferences. I allocate more time to quiet writing as the year progresses and students become engrossed in their work. This activity sets a calm, focused tone for the rest of the workshop. At the end of the writing period, I discuss procedure, lead students through a writing exercise, or demonstrate how I craft my own stories. These lessons vary in length from five to forty-five minutes, depending on our purposes. We then move into twenty-minute small- or whole-group shares. In small-group shares, students write a story together or respond to each other's work. In whole-group shares, the class addresses the concerns of an individual writer.

On a dry erase board at the front of the room, I post a schedule for the workshop, including the title of the daily lesson. A clearly labeled Writers' Center occupies a corner of the room near the board. At a table, writers find ruled paper, pencils, a pencil sharpener, black fine-line illustration pens, rulers, colored pencils, markers, a pad of Post-it notes, a jar filled with student name tags for a sign-up chart, and clear plastic covers for published books. A Read Me in-box sits next to the paper holder. A student who wants my comments, thinks a story is ready for editing, or has other concerns writes the issue on a Post-it note and puts the piece in the box. I read these stories nightly and write my comments on another Post-it note or ask the student for a conference. This simple procedure helps prioritize my time. Often I don't need to meet face-to-face with a student; quick notes move some writers along while leaving time for me to confer with those whose concerns require interaction and dialogue.

A pocket chart hangs next to the table. The chart functions as a flexible sign-up for student–teacher conferences, whole-group shares, word processing time at the classroom computer, and author's celebrations. I label the four functions on the chart, and students insert a laminated name tag to sign up for an activity. They remove the tag once they have completed a

- Writing Paper
- Pencils
- Electric Pencil Sharpener
- Fine-line Black Pens
- Colored Pencils and Markers
- Rulers
- Clear Plastic Covers
- Post-it Notes
- Jar Holding Name Tags
- "Read Me" Box

FIG. 1–1: *What to Include at a Writing Center*

task. This easy system encourages writers to take charge of their writing process by evaluating their progress and deciding what to do next.

Each writer also maintains a daily writing folder, a Thinking About Fiction notebook, and a storage file. Students keep the daily writing folder at their desk. These folders hold two or three stories in progress, a personalized spelling dictionary, and the fiction notebook. The notebook is a ruled school-issued composition book that fits into the pocket of the folder. We use the notebook to record observations, rewrite story sections, and document other whole-group writing exercises. The storage file is kept in a crate at the center. I set up a file for each student at the beginning of the year. The file holds abandoned and set-aside pieces. Writers store and retrieve work on their own, but periodically I ask the class to sort through daily folders to find stories to set aside. This culling keeps daily folders manageable and students focused on a few important pieces.

Once students decide to publish, they request a Peer Response Record. The record helps writers keep track of shares and allows me to review stories early on in the process. I ask four questions before I give the record to a writer: Is this a verbatim retelling from a book, TV, movie, or video game? Does this piece contain swearing, cussing, or "toilet talk?" If there's

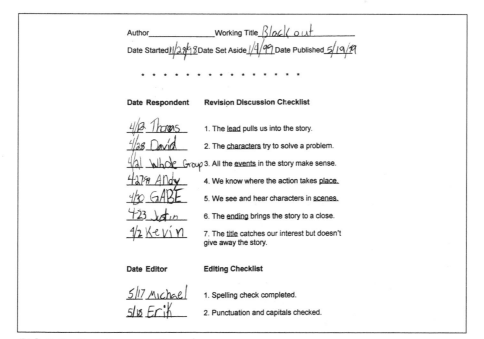

FIG. 1–2: Peer Response Record

violence, does it serve a purpose? Is this the best first draft the writer can produce right now?

The *language* standard reflects my interpretation of community values, and students usually understand the need to use *appropriate language* in stories. After all, parents and neighbors read our work at Open House. However, fifth-graders aren't always sure about violence. Movies and TV are full of it. Boys, especially, like to lop off arms and heads in bloody haunted house chases and superhero fights. Thomas Newkirk (2000, 299) argues this is "part of the cultural material that boys (and many girls) bring into the classroom," suggesting that much of it "is like 'violence with a wink,' violence that parodies itself or at least suggests its own reality." This argument makes sense to me, but like all story elements, violent events should serve a narrative purpose. I talk to authors about this, and if we can't justify including violence, I ask them to rewrite, modifying or deleting words, phrases, and sentences that clutter the plot and distract the reader.

I send media retellings back to writers and ask them to add original events and characters. I look for a balance in these revised pieces, a mix of new and borrowed ideas. When I evaluate whether the draft represents the writer's best work, I consider the writer's development, previous stories, the time of year, and how the student feels about the piece. Story length usually isn't an issue. First drafts vary from one to twenty handwritten pages, depending on the piece and the author. In September most stories are two to four pages long. They're longer by the spring as students gain confidence and acquire fluency. I don't expect each piece to be longer and/or better than the last but usually hold writers to a higher standard in April than I do in October, challenging them to grow and to develop their skills.

Writers use the Peer Response Record for about a week, selecting respondents to discuss and sign off each checklist item. This process ensures feedback from a wide range of viewpoints. Students talk about beginnings or *leads*, story conflicts, story logic, setting, scene writing, endings, and titles, applying ideas they've learned in lessons and in conferences. They sometimes spend weeks revising pieces before they're ready for publication.

Editing comes last, after writers complete the record, share with peers, confer with me, and revise the story. Students check spelling and punctuation with one another, recording completion on the Peer Response Record. They also use a Spelling Check and a personal dictionary during this process. Writers circle suspicious words in the draft and list them in the first column on the Spelling Check. Often the second guess, written in the next column, is closer to convention than the first. They use a dictionary or work with me in an editing conference to fill in the final spelling in the third column. Students transfer the correct spelling to the

Suspicious Word	Second Guess	Final Spelling
Glimese	Glimes	glimpse
Clouser	closer ✓	closer
Tighter ✓	Thighter	tighter
Hurracane	Hurracaine	hurricane
Stream ✓	Strem	stream
Choclate	Chocolate ✓	chocolate
Peppermint ✓	Pepermint	peppermint
Vinilla	Vannilla	vanilla
Startled ✓	Startled	startled
Stumbled ✓	Stumbloed	stumbled
Souckked	Socked ✓	soaked
Leaves ✓	Leavfed	leaves
Surronded	Surrounded ✓	Surrounded

BACK ↵

FIG. 1–3: *Spelling Check*

story and to an alphabetized personal dictionary that they keep for future reference.

In summary then, a story starts during quiet write. In shares, writers decide whether or not to publish a piece. If they decide not to publish, they place the story in the Storage File. If they decide to publish, they request a Peer Response Record by placing the piece in the Read Me box. I review the stories and respond with comments and/or give the students the response record. The students then find respondents to discuss issues on the checklist. If students feels stuck, they sign up for a whole-group share or write a note and put the piece in the Read Me box again. I give a quick written response or conduct further one-on-one discussions. We do a final pre-editing conference to decide whether the story is ready for publication. Once we decide, the writer receives the Spelling Check, edits, types, and illustrates the story.

Students write an About the Author to include at the end of the book. I used to ask them to write about themselves, about favorite stories, things

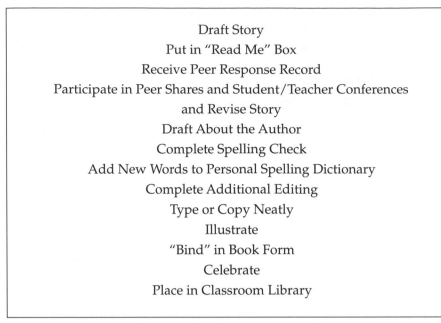

FIG. 1–4: *Publishing a Story*

they like to do, brothers and sisters. Now they write about writing the story because this encourages metacognition and self-evaluation. Where did you get the idea for this story? Where did you get stuck? How did you solve the problem? Who helped you on this story? What did they do to help? What do you like best about the story? Why? How long did it take to write? How does this story compare with other stories you've written? I want students to reflect as they write, with the hope that they will become as sophisticated and thoughtful as Lori, who wrote the following About the Author after completing "Land Under the Bathtub."

> Lori got the idea for her book when she was trying to help Cindy. Cindy came up with an idea about a girl that takes a bath and turns into a boy. That's when it came into Lori's head that there could be a little land under the bathtub.
> At first when she started writing "The Land Under the Bathtub" she was going to write that Susan was going to have a war with the ugliest flower in the world. Then she wanted to write that she had trouble making friends. Finally, she decided that she could write a series about the land under the bathtub.

She wants to thank Susan for helping her think about how to end this story because she was stuck on it for a long time. She also wants to thank Cindy for giving her the idea for this story.

She thinks this story is her best one because she spent a lot of time on it. This is her fourth published book in fifth grade.

We honor students' published books in an Author's Celebration during Readers' Workshop. The author sits in a chair as we sit in a circle on the carpet. After the author reads the story, we offer praise, telling what we like about the piece. This is a big moment for students. They work very hard on revisions and deserve the compliments. After the celebration the writer places the book in the classroom library on a special rack with slots labeled and set aside for each author's work. The book becomes a resource for daily reading and a continual reminder that we write for one another.

TALKING ABOUT STORIES

Talking about stories drives the workshop. Talk occurs in lessons, conferences, and shares. I set the tone and model ways to talk about fiction in group lessons and in one-on-one conferences. Whereas lessons present ideas, conferences provide ways to tailor these ideas to the needs of individual students. Writers try out talking about stories in small- and whole-group peer shares.

Lessons

Lessons provide opportunities to present a wide range of material in a short period of time, but every time I give a lesson, I'm aware of the jumpy, unfocused kids, the ones who don't eat breakfast, fiddle with dinosaur erasers, or can't listen, so I don't expect mastery. I see a lesson as a beginning, a way to introduce ideas that we'll come back to over and over again.

I give lessons on workshop procedure, editing, and elements of fiction. Procedural lessons focus on practical issues like using the Peer Response Record, the Spelling Check, or the personal dictionary. Sometimes a lesson reminds students about publishing procedures or behavior in peer shares. At the beginning of the year I spend time talking about word processing, including how to format and print stories. In editing lessons I look for error patterns in student writing and teach paragraphing, quotation marks, commas, capitalization, and other appropriate conventions.

I spend most of our lesson time exploring the elements of fiction, which include characters, settings, plot, titles, and endings. Lessons on elements fall into three categories, distinguished partly by purpose but mainly by the ways in which students participate in the discussions: (1) In *exercises* I teach an element and students immediately respond, practicing it in writing; (2) In *demonstrations* I model thinking by writing a short piece and asking students for comments, (3) In *pattern lessons* I ask writers how they typically approach a story element. Then we collate and evaluate their responses, looking for writing patterns common to the class. Exercises, demonstrations, and pattern lessons support and reinforce one another. Exercises provide direct instruction and immediate practice; demonstrations show subtle links between thinking and writing; pattern lessons help students understand how they write.

Each writing exercise teaches a specific element of fiction. These exercises define elements while providing techniques for improving the use of these components in stories. I begin the year with a series of lessons using the senses to write scenes. I follow this with lessons on characterization, asking writers to observe kids at school and write short pieces incorporating what they learn about appearance, action, and dialogue. I also teach ways to craft beginnings, to show setting, or to define story conflicts. In an exercise on beginnings or leads, for instance, students rewrite the first paragraph of a novel I've read to the class or write the beginning of a story we create as a group. We compare our leads, discussing ways to engage readers in the first few sentences of a piece. These exercises provide direct instruction and immediate story writing practice.

I work with my stories in demonstration lessons, focusing the discussion on a particular issue. As I write I think out loud, modeling how I construct ideas as I create the piece. In the following lesson I revised the lead to my "Seven Frogs" story, revealing my reasons as I rewrote sentences on the transparency.

> I've been thinking about how to start my story. . . . I want to start with dialogue so I can introduce one of the characters right away. I want the dialogue to show how excited she is and, this way, also excite the reader . . . so I'll start by saying:
>
> *I wrote:*
>
> "There's one, I'll reach over the rock and get it." Judy propped her bare foot against a smooth log lying across the creek bed. Just as she cupped both hands over the unsuspecting frog, Susan spotted another one a few feet away.

I don't know if I like the dialogue. She doesn't sound very excited. I think I'll change the second sentence into action because if she says only "There's one!" it sounds like she's more excited, like she's so excited she doesn't waste time <u>saying</u> what she's going to do; she just does it. But I'll need to make sure that my new sentence includes the part about reaching over the rock because telling the reader about the rock gives information about where this first scene takes place. So I'll change it to say:

I wrote:

"There's one!" Judy reached over the rock, propping her bare foot against a smooth log lying across the creek bed. . . .

I began this demonstration by telling why the character talks in the first sentence. After I drafted the lead, I thought out loud, deciding to strengthen the character's voice by shortening the dialogue. I told students that I wanted to convert talk to action without losing details that show setting. I write; I think; I rewrite. In demonstration lessons like this, I show how writers mull over ideas as they discover a story.

In pattern lessons we brainstorm ways fifth-graders commonly write titles, endings, leads, dialogue, character introductions, and other fiction elements. We summarize what kids do, discovering how young writers usually think about these issues. It always amazes me how easy this process is for kids, but they come to know their habits as they read one another's stories in peer shares and during readers' workshop. In a typical pattern lesson on leads, for instance, hands pop up all over the room as writers eagerly contribute the beginning lines from one of their stories. We discuss the leads and look for patterns—such as listing all the characters' names in the first sentence. I sometimes begin the study of an element with information like this, showing students what they do before we look carefully at other ways of writing. I also use pattern lessons at the end of the year to bring closure to the workshop. In May or early June we look back at our writing, summarizing the genres and themes that emerged from our stories. Pattern lessons encourage metacognition, raising consciousness about what students write and how they think.

Conferences

A conference is a bridge linking what students and teachers know about fiction. When I speak one-on-one with a writer, I bring to the conversation my understanding of how to tell a story. Students do the same. My job is to find a common ground, to ask questions that link the writer's experience to classroom discussions while staying open to his or her unique ways of working with fiction. In conferences, we draw from our collective understanding to negotiate solutions to story issues.

There's an art to negotiating a good writing conference. It requires weighing what I know about fiction, what I know about the writer, and what I see in the piece we are discussing. I act as an alter ego, modeling ways to think about fiction as I monitor my talk and the writer's response. The dialogue raises issues and/or confirms what writers already know but haven't named or discussed with others. I write suggestions or questions on Post-its to help students remember our discussions after they leave conferences to begin revisions. They keep these notes, creating an ongoing record of our conversations that I use to refresh my memory each time we meet.

I conduct four types of conferences, each with a special purpose: fiction conferences focus on elements of story writing; process conferences help writers understand how they go about writing; evaluation conferences explore what writers think about their work; and editing conferences help them see how they use conventions and syntax to communicate stories.

I ask certain types of questions in each of these conferences. When I conduct a process conference, I usually begin with an open-ended question like "How did you go about writing this piece?" Depending on the response, I follow up with:

Did you have any problems with this piece?
How did you solve the problem?
Who helped you on this piece?
What did they do?
What was the easiest part to write? Why?
How long did it take you to write it?
How does this compare with other pieces you've written?

In evaluation conferences, I use a similar strategy, beginning the dialogue with "What do you think about this piece?" and continuing with more specific questions:

Is there a part in this piece that you really like?
Why do you like it?
If you could revise this piece, what would you do?
What do readers think about your piece?
How does this piece compare to other stories you've written?

When I edit with writers, I go over the Spelling Check and quickly look for patterns in syntax and conventions. I spend a long time editing with ELL students, or English Language Learners. We look at verb tenses, verb/subject agreement, use of articles and prepositions, and other syntactical issues common to writers acquiring English.

Fiction writing conferences present the greatest challenge for me. I focus on seven story elements: characterization, setting, plot, scene writing, leads, and endings. These are complex issues, so I take them a step at a time, discussing one problem in each conference. If a student has a long story with multiple problems, it may take three or four conferences to work through the piece. I prioritize these problems, focusing on the fundamental issues first. When I hear a piece, I listen for a clear, focused plot, a sound story foundation. If this is weak or missing, the writer and I explore a problem for the characters to solve. We also address illogical or unclear event sequences or *plot jumps*, putting ourselves in the place of the characters and clarifying the action. If a piece contains too much talking, we tackle that next. Then, if necessary, we rethink front-loaded information, discussing how to rewrite the first page without giving away the ending, listing all the characters' names, or providing other information that's better sprinkled throughout the body of the story. Finally, we work on skillfully adding details to show characters and setting. The writer leaves these conferences with a specific task, suggestion, or idea written on a reminder Post-it. Once the story is revised, the author puts the piece in the Read Me box again and continues to confer with me and with peers until we've solved most problems and agree that the story makes sense.

For many years I resisted offering advice to writers, believing that they discovered what they needed indirectly through my questions. I trusted that my queries led to thoughtful reflections, and if they didn't, I assumed that writers weren't ready for them. I don't believe this anymore. Writers

---

No Story Focus

Plot Jumps

Too Much Talking

Frontloading Information

Flat Characters

Placelessness

FIG. 1–5: Prioritizing Common Story Writing Problems

come to conferences with varying skills, learning styles, understandings, motivation, and experience. Some listen to my questions, reflect, and go back to their desks able to construct meaningful revisions on their own; others need direct advice. Thus, during a conference I continually monitor a writer's response, asking myself: Should I tell the writer what I see in this piece or should I approach the issue indirectly, posing a question that leads him or her to discover a problem? How many issues should we tackle? Should I give specific revision advice, or should I let the writer come up with a solution?

Monitoring the writer's response requires active listening, flexible thinking, and careful talk. The process is like a dance: you pose a question; the writer responds, moving one way; you listen and respond, moving in the same direction. Because you're the lead, you subtly change course and see if the writer follows. If the question confuses, you slip back to something more familiar, try the move again, this time varying the step ever so slightly. A good example of this process occurred in a conference with Paulo. I was trying to help him convert dialogue into action in his "Night of the Living Toys" story. A few minutes into our conversation I changed the direction of our talk as I noticed his growing confusion:

Paulo read his piece, which began:

One day two boys were playing.
    "Hey, let's go get the tent, OK?"
    "OK."
    "Mom, where's the tent?"
    "It's in your room."
    "OK, come on, let's go."
    "OK."
    They went and got the tent.
    "Hey, what's that noise?"
    "AHHHHHHHHHH. The toys came alive!"
    "Run!"
    "OK."
    "AHHHHHHH. Wolverine got me. AHHHHHHH."

MS. J: What do you think about the dialogue in this piece?

PAULO: It's good. . . .

MS. J: How about the amount of dialogue?

PAULO: A lot of it?

MS. J: I think so. Do you remember the lesson last week? We talked about what to do when you have too much talking.

PAULO: You're supposed to make it longer?

MS. J: Make it longer? What do you mean?

PAULO: Like, make it longer . . . about the dialogue?

MS. J: You make the dialogue longer?

PAULO: No . . . 'cause there's too much talking.

MS. J: Let's look at your piece and underline the dialogue.

Paulo underlined the dialogue.

PAULO: . . . it was too much right there and right here. . .

MS. J: Yes, there's too much dialogue. One way to change it is to turn some of the dialogue into action. Let's go through your story and double underline the talking that shows how the characters feel about each other. That's the dialogue you'll keep. The rest you'll change into a description of action.

I began the conference with an open-ended question about dialogue, hoping Paulo would notice that his piece contained too much talking. But his response told me otherwise, so I narrowed the question and asked him directly. Once he identified the problem, I probed to see if he remembered our dialogue discussion the week before. I could tell by his response that he either wasn't listening or didn't understand the lesson. I switched my talk at this point, refocusing Paulo on the piece and then directly telling him what I thought he needed to do to improve this part of his story.

Usually students initiate conferences by inserting their name in the pocket chart. Under certain circumstances, however, I ask for one. If I suggest a revision, I ask writers to sign up for a follow-up talk to discuss the rewrite. I also ask for a conference if I can't respond adequately in writing to a student's request for comments in my Read Me box. Periodically I ask to speak to "private" writers, the ones who shy away from conferences and work quietly on their own. Often these students are stuck and don't know how to ask for help.

Shares

Shares are small- or whole-group settings where students write collaboratively or share a piece and ask for feedback. Shares underscore that writing is a social act, a communication of ideas between reader and writer. Shares help writers apply ideas and provide opportunities to socialize, encouraging the discovery of stories as students converse.

Writers share pieces with the whole workshop, in small groups, or with partners. We sit in a big circle on the carpet for whole-group shares. These discussions furnish students with a wide range of responses and reinforce the idea that we work together as a community of writers. Small-group and partner shares are held at tables, on the carpet, and in other places around the room. These intimate discussions afford students a safe, comfortable venue in which to explore story ideas.

Writers work with partners or in small groups to discuss issues on the Peer Response Record, to conduct unstructured student-initiated shares, or to write a story collaboratively. These shares serve a variety of purposes. Peer Response shares help writers apply ideas from lessons and conferences; student-initiated shares encourage authors to identify writing problems and guide the talking; collaboration shares provide time for students to write a story with another author. All small-group shares create a sense of audience, allowing writers to test ideas and assess the responses of potential readers in a small, safe setting.

For a long time I resisted using a peer-response record to structure small groups, believing that my agendas encroached on the writers' sense of ownership and thereby stifled creativity. I used to encourage students to make comments but didn't interfere by suggesting topics or discussion items. However, I found that if I leave shares totally unstructured, students don't talk about many of the issues I raise in our group discussions. Fiction writing is extremely difficult, and using the record encourages students to use and internalize the complex ideas I introduce.

When writers discuss items on the Record, the conversation is short and focused. Sandy and Lori discussed Sandy's "Too Tall for Jenny" a few days after they helped Jessica. In the share, they addressed scene writing:

Sandy read her first scene:

"We only have five minutes before the game starts," Jenny said. Jenny was our center, so she was the tallest girl on the team. She wore her hair in a long brown pony tail everyday.

"I think I'm going to be sick. We're never going to win because we're not used to playing together and it's our first game," I said to Jenny.

"I don't think I am going to be able to play," said Jenny.

Me and Jenny were standing side by side looking at the girls on the other team and watching them shoot to see how good they were.

"Oh, no, Jenny, look at their center. She's way bigger than you."

"I bet she will get the jump ball," Jenny said.

"I hear she broke a kid's arm by swatting it so hard. I have to stay on their guard. She looks really good." I whispered.

"Man, we're going to get creamed," Maya said.

The whistle blew. It was time for the jump ball.

SANDY: OK, what do you think? Is it a good scene, I mean can you hear and see the characters?

LORI: Yeah, like the two girls, like just standing around looking at people playing basketball.

SANDY: Well, do you think it's a scene? I mean does it sound like one?

LORI: Yeah, it has action and dialogue.

SANDY: And I put in description, like when I say that they're standing side by side.

LORI: Yeah, that's a scene.

Sandy and Lori defined a scene as they evaluated the piece. They agreed that scenes contain dialogue and action. Drawing on previous lessons and conferences, they tried out ideas and discovered how scene writing applied to their work. The talk was concise, focusing on one important fiction element.

Student-initiated, unstructured shares usually occur while authors are writing a first draft. They use the share to try out or brainstorm ideas. They make up the rules and guide the talk, reinforcing ownership and independence. I ask them to use clipboards and record the date, the respondent's name and comments, and the working title of the piece. They staple their notes to the back of the story. This procedure keeps writers accountable and helps them remember questions and suggestions when they revise.

Dialogue in kid-initiated shares varies depending upon the mix of students in the group. A writer with a strong sense of purpose controls the talk, keeping the group or partner focused. In the following share, Jessica pursued her agenda, despite some initial confusion:

Jessica read "Pay Back" later retitled "Why Did You Leave?" (see Chapter 4).

A girl was sitting at the park with her mom. Her two sisters were playing with her brother. Her dad was dead. He killed himself. She did not like talking about him so much. The mom did not know how to cope with her husband dead. Her mom said that Sherry looked like her father so much that the mom felt like killing Sherry. Sherry, Michelle, and Nick were scared of their mother. Beth, the mom, Sherry, Jessica, Michelle, and Nick were driving to a new home. They did not want to remember their dad. She felt like a payback.

JESSICA: Do you like the story I wrote at all?

JUDY: Yeah.

JESSICA: Does it make sense?

LORI: Yeah, I think.

JESSICA: Does it go on and on, talking and talking?

[long pause]

SANDY: Will you read the story again?

[Jessica reread the story.]

SANDY: I don't get it when she says she felt like a "payback."

JESSICA: That's what Olivia wrote. It's like she felt like paying him back.

SANDY: I don't understand it. What about the dad? I don't get it when the dad kills himself.

JESSICA: He kills himself. . . . see the thing that we did at first was kind of confusing, so we wrote it over again. We didn't put all of the details back in this part of the story.

SANDY: Aren't they sad? Don't they care?

JESSICA: Yeah, they're sad, that's why we put . . . oh, we never put that, we didn't finish writing. . . .

LORI: I think it needs more details.

Jessica clearly controlled this share. She initiated the conversation by asking if kids liked her story. She rephrased her question two times before someone in the group requested a rereading, then she dialogued with Sandy until the two of them discovered accidental deletions and parts of the story that needed more detail.

Most kids love collaboration shares, the social act of creating a story with another writer. In fact, some would spend all their time collaborating if I didn't limit these shares to partner time, saving quiet write for stories they create on their own. I monitor this allocation of time because when kids write together, they don't always struggle with the full spectrum of fiction writing issues. They find comfortable roles as they interact: storytellers provide ideas; composers write sentences; illustrators create drawings; and editors weed out misspellings and add capitals and punctuation. Kids tend to prefer one role over another, but roles sometimes change from group to group and from one time to the next.

In the following collaboration, Linda and Hien brainstormed ideas for a new story, each equally participating in the storytelling, but Linda clearly anticipated illustrating as she negotiated with her partner:

HIEN: How about: There was a dog, and he was walking along, and he was crying?

LINDA: Two dogs were crying. How about a person in it?

HIEN: A person kills another person. No, that's too violent.

LINDA: We could make it a dog.

HIEN: Or birds? About birds and dogs?

LINDA: Yeah, why don't we write about a bird? He couldn't fly and then this dog came along over there and, like, helped him, so he won't get hurt.

HIEN: Or a robot hamster that can talk! [giggles]

LINDA: I can't draw that.

HIEN: OK, so let's write about birds and dogs saving each other. What's the title?

LINDA: "Birdie and Doggie."

HIEN: No, let's make up their names.

I keep a low profile during partner shares but set clear standards at the beginning of the year. I role play an unstructured share during the first few weeks of class. In the role play I model a process, suggesting that the writer identify the reason for the share, ask for questions and comments, and close by telling the respondent what he or she plans to do next. Sometimes I circulate from share to share, monitoring student talk. I intervene only when a pair seems stuck or is wasting too much time.

We follow a similar process in whole-group shares. Writers tell the reason for the share and read the piece. The audience questions and comments while a recorder takes notes. The share ends with the writer's reflections. I facilitate these discussions to move the exchange along or to refocus energy. I participated at two points in Susan's share, once to calm the group and again to raise an important issue. Susan shared "Wash Up," a story about a girl who takes a bath and slowly turns into a boy:

SUSAN: I need help . . . if she sounds like a boy or not.

Susan read the piece:

"Mary, time for your bath," Mary's mother screamed.

"Do I have to?" Mary asked running into her mother's room.

"Yes, you're not getting out of this bath like yesterday," her mother said.

"Fine, you . . . you . . . mean mom!"

Mary stomped into the bathroom and slammed the door shut. She turned the knob to the bathtub until it was just right. She walked over to the sink to brush her teeth. She looked in the little cupboard under the sink.

She couldn't find her toothpaste. Mary looked way in the back. She found something that felt like it. She took it out and she read: "Bubble Boy's Bubble Bath."

"Wow," Mary said to herself, "I get bubble bath."

She forgot about brushing her teeth. She saw how full the bathtub was. She didn't turn the water off, though, because she wanted to put bubble bath in. When she did it foamed to the top. She quickly turned off the water and admired the tub for a moment. The bubble bath was turning green. "Cool, it's green bubble bath," Mary said slowly.

She stepped into the bathtub. It was sort of hot. She slowly slipped into the bubbles and sat down at the bottom of the bathtub.

"Ewwwwwww. This stuff smells like dirt and sweat," Mary said. She quickly took her bath, rushing.

Mary laughed. "Burrrrrrp"

"Excuse me!" Mary's mother said.

But she didn't say it, she just put her dirty old white East Side shoes on the table. Her little sister Sandy dropped Mary's food on the table. Mary could see Sandy's eyes were red from crying.

"Oh, did the little baby cry?" Mary said.

"Oh, Mary, be quiet!" Mary's mother snapped.

"I'm not hungry," Mary said as she walked away.

It was time for school so Mary grabbed her backpack and ran out the door not waiting for her sister to come along. When she got to school, she ran in her class. There she saw Marissa, Judy, Sophia, and Susan walking towards her way. "Wow, Sophia's fine," Mary said with excitement.

At this point, the group giggled and fidgeted.

MS. J.: Some of you feel a little embarrassed by that last line, but let's stay focused to help the writer. This is an interesting piece because a girl turns into a boy. The character changes so much, but the story won't work unless we believe the changes. Susan, read the rest and restate what you want us to talk about before you call on kids.

[Susan read the rest of the story.]

SUSAN: I want to know if you can tell that she's changing into a boy.

SOPHIA: You could tell she was changing by when she said, "Why do I like Sophia."

SANDY: "Fat scrub," she said that.

PAULO: She burped and didn't say excuse me.

AZAR: Right after she gets out of the tub she should say, "I feel weird," or something like that because, like, shouldn't if she changes, like, feel different or something?

MS. J: That's an interesting point, Azar. Sandy, Sophia, and Paulo gave examples of actions that show Mary changing into a boy. Does Susan show us how Mary feels about this?

[long pause]

PATRICK: That sweaty smell, she didn't like it.

MS. J: Anything else?

[pause]

MS. J: What do you think, Susan?

SUSAN: I don't know.

MS. J: Maybe you should write more about her feelings. What does the group think?

MICHELLE: It's kind of weird turning into a boy. [some giggles]

MARISSA: It must feel different, so you should show how she feels.

MS. J: Can you help her with ideas?

The group continued for several minutes, discussing feelings and how to include them in the story.

Susan's piece evoked a lot of energy. After all, her character changes gender. I intervened, acknowledging their discomfort, when the group lost focus. I reiterated that our purpose was to look at how Susan's character changes. Later I intervened again, making a distinction between showing change through actions and through feelings.

I encourage reluctant writers to share when they feel ready. I keep a list of these students and check with them every now and again. Most writers share in whole group by the end of the year. Many gain confidence by sharing in small groups and by observing responses when students select their published stories at reading time.

Shares, conferences, and lessons are the fabric of the workshop. In the chapters that follow, I weave these components into a process for teaching fiction writing to youngsters. I begin in Chapter 2 by focusing on scenes to introduce character-centered fiction. In Chapter 3 I discuss learning to observe like a writer, helping young authors take the first step toward rethinking character presentation. Chapter 4 explores the craft of creating characters who talk, move, and feel. Finally, Chapter 5 describes conferences and lessons that help writers refine plot and setting, discover themes, and evaluate craft.

2

Starting with the Scene

Good Writers Know
Characters drive stories.
Characters interact in specific places.
Scenes show characters interacting.

CHARACTER-DRIVEN FICTION

I use scene writing to introduce ten-year-olds to character-driven fiction. In a well-written scene, we watch as characters move, talk, and show what they think and how they feel. Authors thoughtfully place scenes throughout a piece, slowing down the narrative and allowing us, for a moment, to see the story as if it were a movie. Scenes show the fictional world in rich, life-like detail. As Burke and Tinsley (1993 152–153) explain, "A scene is showing instead of telling what's happening, a mini-drama with a climax, a vivid rendering of one time and place."[1]

Scene writing forces young authors to "get inside" characters to "enter as participants the situation (they've) created" (Burke and Tinsley 1993, 152). Scene writing also addresses two other fiction writing problems. When left to work on their own, ten-year-olds "tell" a story, and each event seems just as important as the next. Scene writing teaches students to "show not tell" and helps them evaluate events as they ponder whether to write a scene or not.

Like everything else, learning to write scenes is a long, slow, recursive process. It takes some kids a year or two to internalize our conferences and lessons. Others learn it quickly. Thus, if I teach most students to develop characters, evaluate events, and *show* a story, I've tackled something significant. Ten-year-olds are ready to look at these issues, and scene writing is an excellent way to begin.

SKITS AS SCENES

I begin our study with role plays, two-minute impromptu skits to help writers see that action and dialogue drive stories. Students select a partner, make up two characters, and define a setting and a problem for the characters to solve. They don't write dialogue but practice the skit before performing for the class. After the performance, students write the skit as if it were a short dramatic story. In Emily and Mindy's drama, two bored girls stick tape on their faces while hanging out in a mother's bedroom. Patrick and Ronnie's "Bud" and "Clevis" try unsuccessfully to fix a car on a deserted dirt road. Both pairs arrived at these scenarios after five to ten minutes of animated brainstorming. In the following conversation, Joseph and Peter worked through several possibilities before settling on a "World War" scene:

PETER: You act stupid like. . . .
JOSEPH: Yeah, I act stupid. I'll do dumb stuff.
PETER: You'll be Kevin.
JOSEPH: I know, Stupido!
PETER: Can't be Stupido.
JOSEPH: OK, Kevin.
PETER: He's tall. No, he scrubs a lot.
JOSEPH: Did you put in that he's stupid, always acts stupid?
PETER: Yeah, he's always stupid, like [puts his finger in his mouth and crosses his eyes; they laugh]. Oh, and I'm smarter but I make a joke out of everything.
JOSEPH: OK, you're Joe.
PETER: Hey, I know, I'm trying to get you out of this house like in my story.
JOSEPH: No, we're in the supermarket and we get lost.
PETER: No, I'll make it up.
JOSEPH: OK, but you do something to me. But I'm stupid. I know, we skateboard and I scrub. I'll say, "Man, I keep scrubbing."
PETER: You don't say anything, you just do stupid things.
JOSEPH: Hey it's the sixties. . . .

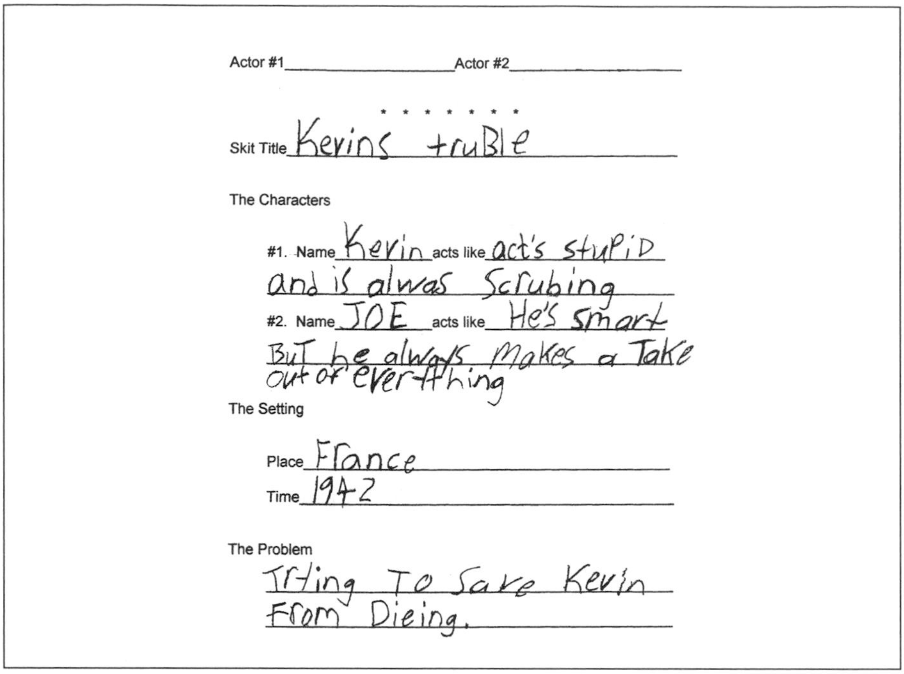

Actor #1_____ Actor #2_____

. . . .

Skit Title *Kevins truBle*

The Characters

#1. Name *Kevin* acts like *act's stuPiD and is alwas Scrubing*

#2. Name *JOE* acts like *He's smart BuT he always makes a Jake out of everything*

The Setting

Place *France*
Time *1942*

The Problem
Trting To Save Kevin From Dieing.

FIG. 2–1: *Scenes as Skits*

PETER: Or we could be in World War Two!
JOSEPH: Yeah, I get shot in the heart.
PETER: No, no, we see this land mine and you think it's a lump . . .
JOSEPH: And I step on it. . . .
PETER: Yeah, but I try to keep you. I say, "Watch that! Watch that!"
JOSEPH: I'm dumb. I say, "Oh, it's just a lump."

Joseph and Peter tried out dialogue and imagined action as they sorted through ideas for their skit. They established the characters' relationship at the beginning of the conversation and then rejected three ideas before settling on the minefield scenario. After the performance some students captured the essential talk and movement of this role play. Jennifer described "Kevin's Troubles" this way:

Kevin scrubbed. "You're a freaken [*sic*] scrub, man," Joe said. Then Kevin saw a bump. "Bumpy, bumpy!" Kevin went running to it. Then Joe grabbed him, "It's a bomb, man, it's a bomb." Joe said.

Kevin started slapping Joe. Kevin got free, but before he could get to it, Joe grabbed him. "Do not go near that thing. It's a bomb!" "I don't care. I still want to stomp on it." Kevin said. "But it's a bomb. If you stomp on it, me and you are going to blow up!" Joe said. "So?" Kevin said. Kevin got free, stomped on it, and died.

Other write-ups contained either mostly dialogue or vague summaries of the action, sometimes confusing actors and characters, like Carlos did:

John fell. Kevin said, "Get up, you scrubbed." Then Joseph took John's hand and swing [*sic*] him around and around. Then John swing [*sic*] Joseph around. John blew up because he stepped on a land mine.

Carlo's "scene" had a long way to go, but "Kevin's Troubles" and similar skits provided a launch, a lively introduction to the notion that scenes are dramas driven by characters who talk, move, and explore a made-up world.

STORY TRIPS

Story trips are neighborhood walks that underscore the idea that scenes take place in specific settings. Story trips also encourage authors to use their senses when they write. We go through the same activities on each outing: we walk to a nearby place, sit, close our eyes, and listen. After a few minutes, we smell the air, look around, and touch nearby objects. We complete observations in ten minutes, recording in our fiction notebooks what we hear, smell, see, and touch. We take a few minutes to sketch the place and then write a scene with dialogue, action, and setting details. When we return to class, we discuss our scenes before writing a second draft.

Last year we went to the beach, to a park, to a downtown street, to a residential neighborhood, and to a shopping center; each setting offered different smells, sounds, and sights. Scenes improve over time as students hone observational skills and learn to use sense impressions to create these small character-driven dramas.

On our first few outings we record observations in four boxes labeled Sounds Like, Looks Like, Smells Like, and Feels Like. Depending on the maturity of the group, I sometimes ask students to start by writing one-character scenes in the first person, a natural point of view for authors emerging from the *I* of personal narrative. We change these stories to third person when we revise the scene in class. By our third or fourth trip, most students need less

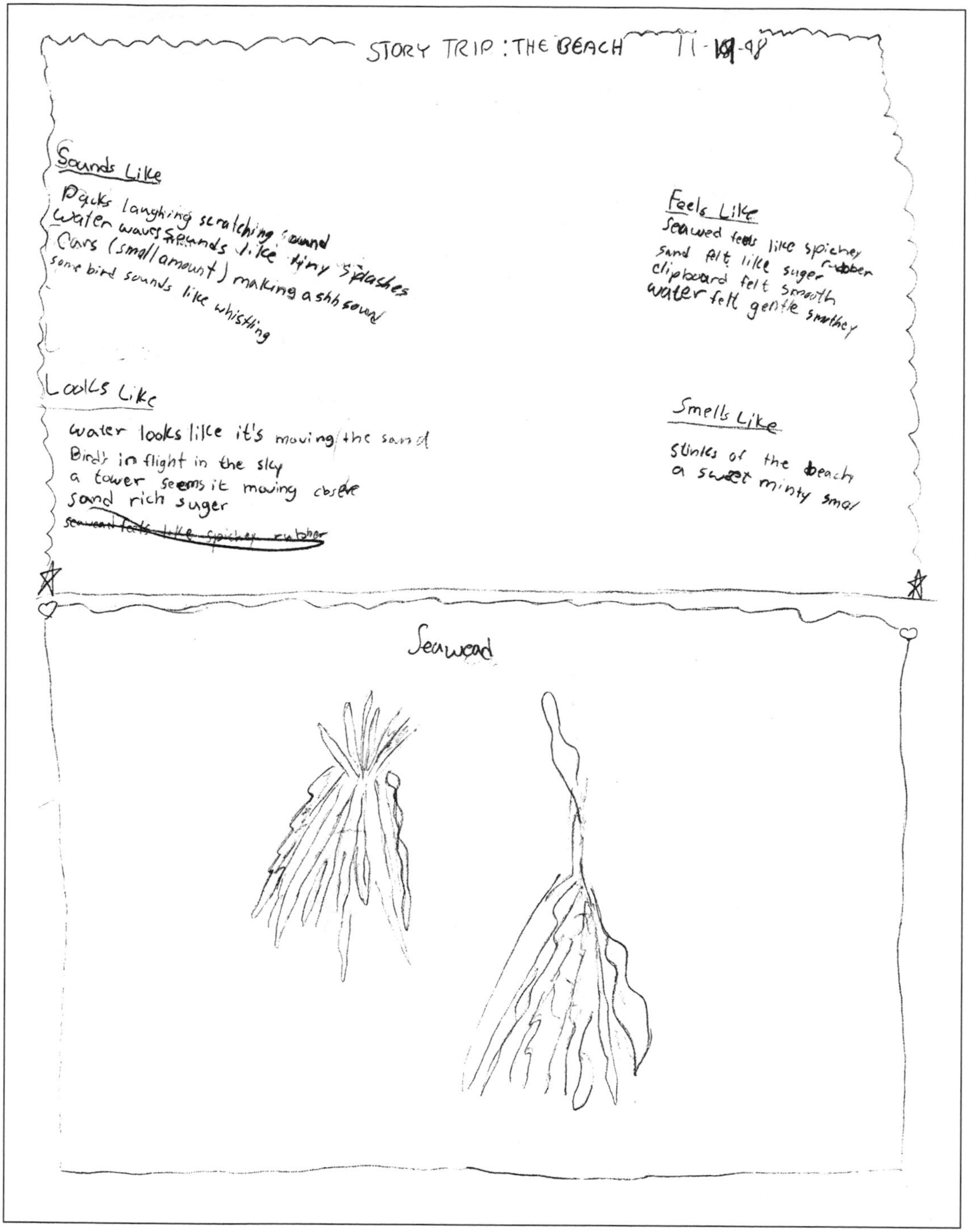

STORY TRIP: THE BEACH   11-19-98

Sounds Like
Ducks laughing scratching sound
water waves sounds like tiny splashes
Oars (small amount) making a shh sound
some bird sounds like whistling

Feels Like
Seaweed feels like spichey rubber
sand felt like suger
clipboard felt smooth
water felt gentle smothey

Looks Like
water looks like it's moving the sand
Birds in flight in the sky
a tower seems it moving closer
sand rich suger
seaweed feels like spichey rubber

Smells Like
stinks of the beach
a sweet minty smell

Seaweed

FIG. 2–2: Information Organizer for Story Trips

structure and can write two-character scenes in the third person without recording observations first. It's recursive learning: we step back and repeat activities, each time *revisiting* scenes in more and more complicated ways.

Students struggle when they create a scene for the first time. Some can't connect actions to make a scene sound like a story. These young writers convert observations into a list of unrelated events much like their skit write-ups and the first drafts of their bed-to-bed personal narratives, which begin in the morning, chronicle a series of events, and end when the writer goes to sleep. In these stories, "each part of the day has equal value" (Graves 1994, 68). Beth's first attempt is a good example. In her beach scene, she listed smells, sounds, and tactile observations in the same way she listed rides at Disneyland in a story written earlier in the year:

> James was walking to the beach and when James was walking James smelled the water. It smelled like rotten egg. Then James looked and seen [*sic*] a duck and one sounded like it was laughing. James heard Susan scream because a bee was after her. Last but not least, James felt the sand. It felt like a slimy worm. James was play fighting with James's friend Tony. She spinned [*sic*] James around.

Repeating story trips over and over again and discussing scenes each time we return to class provides a structure for students to improve scenes

First Trip	Practice in class
	Gather data using organizer
	Write one-character scene in first person
	Discuss and rewrite in third person
Second Trip	Gather data using organizer
	Write one-character scene in first person
	Discuss and rewrite in third person
Third Trip	Organizer optional
	Write two-character scene in third person
	Discuss and rewrite

FIG. 2–3: Sequencing Story Trip Activities

over the course of four or five weeks. Beth's fourth attempt at scene writing sounded more like narrative. Her second draft of a scene at the park shows two characters talking and playing together. We watch as they move from the sand to the swings, discussing how the San Francisco Bay smells "rotten."

> Jessica said, "Olivia, let's go play in the sand." Olivia jumped and got sand in Jessica's eye. "What's that smell?" "That's the Bay. It smells rotten. Do you want to go on the swings? It stinks over here." "Yeah, OK." While they were walking, Jessica stopped to tie her shoes. She told Olivia to go ahead of her and Olivia went. They went on the swings. When Olivia got really high in the air, she jumped off and hurt herself. She saw Jessica still on the swings.

In other first attempts, students omit sense impressions, telling actions but ignoring observations. At the beach, Jacob noticed that waves sound like "a comet hitting the water" and a "washer" and a "hose spraying in the air." In his scene, his character moved in a storylike manner from one action to the next, but he didn't mention the wave or other details from his notebook:

> A man was driving from the city with a boat and was looking for the other island, but it was night. He got lost so he looked for the bowies [sic] to help him and he found the bowie [sic] and found his way and said thanks bowie [sic].

Jacob participated in several more trips and follow-up discussions before incorporating observations into a scene. In his revised draft of a scene set in Washington Park, he showed a boy chasing a squirrel around a tree, adding from his notebook the smell of "pine" and the feel of "slick cool grass."

> Bob ran around trees smelling pine. He saw a squirrel. He crept up behind the squirrel, but the squirrel heard him and darted off. Bob tried to chase the squirrel but tripped over a root and fell on the slick, cool grass.

I notice the same struggle to balance talk and action in these scenes as I notice when students write up skit performances. Jacob's first scene was all action; Beth's first draft of her park scene was all dialogue:

> "Jessica," Olivia said, "Let's go make a sand castle." "Hey, we need some water to make the door." "Okay, Olivia, I'll go to the water

fountain and get some." "Hey, you know what? When I look at this sand it looks like cat litter to me." "You know what? Let's go on the spider web." "From up here I can hear airplanes." "It's getting dark. I have to go home. Bye."

In classroom follow-up discussions, I share my writing and encourage others to do the same. We evaluate our scenes, exploring action, dialogue, and sense impressions. I model ways to talk about scenes: I ask questions and rephrase comments, hoping to provide the language students need to critically evaluate their work. In the following share, we discussed Sophia's scene set in a nearby residential neighborhood. This was Sophia's third attempt at scene writing:

Sophia read her scene:

"It's Halloween night and I'm going to get lots of candy this year!" yelled Marissa in her costume. Lots of kids were out in the night for trick or treating. She came to an old house with tall weeds. She stepped through them and tripped and hurt her foot. A drop hit her head. It was only cracked paint. The window was open and the blinds were whooshing in the wind.

MS. J: What do you think about Sophia's scene?
TONY: It's like she's walking to the house. . . .
STEVEN: And then she trips and walks in the grass and the cracked paint. . . .
MS. J: It sounds like a story. . . . the character is going somewhere.
RICKY: Yeah, maybe in the house.
MS. J: How many characters are in this scene?
SOPHIA: There was someone with her but they don't say anything to each other.
MS. J: Did we hear any sounds in the scene?
STEVEN: The blinds
MS. J: What sound did they make?
STEVEN: Whissing and whooshing . . .

In Sophia's piece, Marissa moves toward the "old house with tall weeds" as if she's beginning a scary journey. Steven heard the connected actions; I reinforced this by saying "the character is going somewhere." I asked about "whooshing" to emphasize how Sophia used sound to show us the blinds.

Eventually, students need to observe the world and write scenes without my guidance. Homework provides additional practice and an opportunity for youngsters to explore scene writing on their own. For several weeks, students replicate story trip activities at home. I ask them to sit in the yard or in the house, make observations, and write a two-character scene. Their scenes improve over several weeks, though many initially have the same difficulties at home as they do on our trips. Some students integrate sense impressions but list random disconnected actions. Others write all dialogue. It often takes three or four story trips, reinforced by home assignments, for students to learn the basic elements of a scene, but once they understand this, they're ready to analyze their daily reading and writing to explore the use of scenes to develop suspense, humor, mystery, and dramatic tension between characters.

READING LIKE A WRITER

Exploring the how and why of scenes in *Bell Prater's Boy* (White 1996), *Bridge to Terabithia* (Paterson 1972), and other well-written novels helps young writers understand the complex and diverse ways that authors use scenes to tell a story. Through guided exposure to good writing, students learn to identify, evaluate, and eventually emulate the scenes others create. The more they know about this subtle and complex craft, the better they write. Good novels provide models for good writing.

Sometimes I simply draw attention to a well-written scene during read-aloud sessions by saying, "Let me read that scene again." At other times we discuss how writers construct scenes. In *On My Honor* we examined how Marion Bauer (1986, 27) used a scene to show competition between Joel and Tony as the two boys struggled against the swift river current just before Tony drowns:

I read the scene, ending with:

"Come on," Tony prodded. "You said out to the sandbar. Are you giving up?" "You sure you'll make it?" Joel eyed his friend's heaving chest meaningfully. "You look pretty tired to me." Tony gave him a shove, almost caught him off balance. "Swim," he commanded, and Joel plunged into the water and resumed swimming.

MS. J: How do Tony and Joel feel about each other in this scene?
OLIVIA: Tony's angry.
SANDY: 'Cause he thinks he can't swim as well.
MS. J: And maybe a little embarrassed. How's Joel feeling?
STEVEN: Happy cause he swims better.
PAULO: Or maybe mad cause he wants Tony to swim better . . .
MS. J: How do we know that Tony is angry?
SUSAN: He shoves and pushes him down and yells at him.

MS. J: We learn that he's angry when the author writes, "Tony gave him a shove, almost caught him off balance. 'Swim,' he commanded."

We continued to discuss the scene for five more minutes.

Most students remember scenes like this long after we finish a book. I sometimes ask them to draw what they recall, and I circulate around the room to confer with them about their illustrations. Students remembered a dozen or so scenes from Elizabeth George Speare's (1983) *Sign of the Beaver*, including the scene in which Matt, a young settler, meets Attean after being stung by swarming bees. In this scene, Matt is stung as he attempts to take honey from a hive hidden in the hollow of a tree. He escapes into the safety of a nearby pond and is rescued by Attean, a young Native American boy. Susan, a strong reader, reconstructed the bee scene with interesting detail, placing a cup and a spoon in Matt's hands because she "remembered that the hole (in the tree) was just big enough for him to put his spoon in." Sophia omitted the pond in her drawing but told me that "Matt was climbing up the tree and he got stung by a whole bunch of bees and he ran and jumped in the water and after that the bees went away and after that Attean and the grandpa came and brought him and he put something on him and after that he took him to his cabin."

Lori's drawing of the fishing scene included a rendering of three fish bones, a broken wooden hook, charred cooking sticks, a fire, Attean's spear, and an anachronistic rod and reel that she imagined Matt owned. She showed Matt frowning because "I always pictured him frowning in the story." She told me she "pictured it out of Matt's eyes. . . . I didn't see Matt but when I saw it, I'm Matt and I'm looking at it. . . . I pictured lots of trees all around. I drew the water different than I pictured it. . . . I saw like little puddles and the pond wasn't really a circle. And there were tiny fish in the puddle and very tall grass around the pond, some parts of it."

We completed the drawing in one or two sessions. As students worked I asked them why the author wrote the scene. Most readers, like Sophia, articulated a purpose.

MS. J: Why did the author make this a scene and not just tell us quickly in a summary?
SOPHIA: Well, because that's how they met. Instead of just saying that, like, the Indian guy just found him, they show he met him. Like, the Indians needed to find him before teaching Attean how to read and then it just goes on and on.
MS. J: If you were to summarize this scene, what would you write?
SOPHIA: Matt got stung by a bunch of bees and fell in the pond and a bunch of Indians came to help him. Attean found him.

FIG. 2–4: Susan's "Bee Scene" from Sign of the Beaver

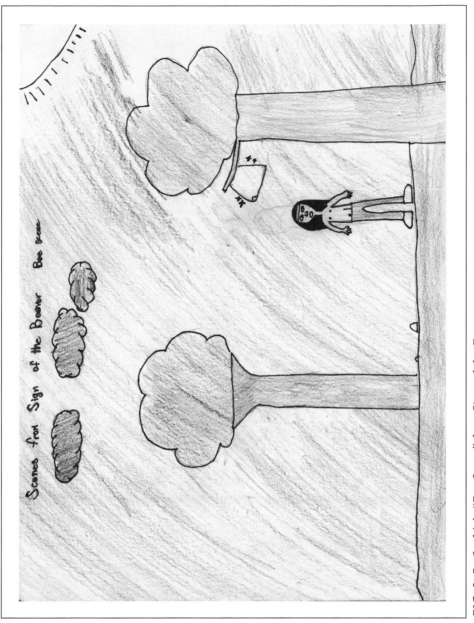

FIG. 2–5: Sophia's "Bee Scene" from Sign of the Beaver

FIG. 2–6: *Lori's "Fishing Scene" from Sign of the Beaver*

Some students couldn't figure this out, so I took a different approach and asked them what the scene shows about the characters, hoping this would clarify the author's intentions.

MS. J: Why do you suppose Elizabeth Speare developed this scene?

JESSICA: Because she thought it would be good to put inside the book?

MS. J: Why is this part of the story important?

JESSICA: Because Matt was showing Attean how to do things and now he wants to show Matt how to do things.

MS. J: What do we learn about the characters in this scene?

JESSICA: Like they're different.

MS. J: What do you mean?

JESSICA: One knows how to catch fish and the other one knows how to read. That Attean can do something that Matt can't. They both can do something the other can't.

MS. J: What do we learn about Matt's feelings in this scene?

JESSICA: He's probably upset because he can't catch a fish. Matt feels upset and Attean feels good.

MS. J: What would you write if you were going to write a summary of this scene?

JESSICA: A summary . . . Attean was going to show Matt how to fish, which Matt couldn't.

MS. J: So what do we learn in the scene that we can't learn from your summary?

JESSICA: The scene shows more. . . . it shows how the people are feeling and what they are doing and a summary just tells about the things.

Readers apply what they learn in these activities to independent reading. Sometimes I ask them to identify a scene during a reading conference. At other times we work as a group and record scenes on a Weekly Reading Focus response sheet. At the end of several weeks of responses, scene drawing, and conferences, students are able to identify scenes in most of the books they read.

DEVELOPING SCENES

Discovering and developing scenes in daily writing is more difficult for students than analyzing scenes in books or writing them as a home assignment or on a story trip. We picture and remember scenes authors create for us in our favorite stories. In a home assignment or on a trip we write an isolated scene and don't worry about the rest of the narrative. Identifying scenes for revision in the stories we write, however, requires that we understand the relative importance of each event—or potential scene—in relation to the story as a whole. Experienced writers weigh events to determine whether the reader needs to hear and see the characters or whether a quick telling will suffice. I can teach this to most fifth-graders; for some, our lessons and conferences introduce a concept they'll come to understand better as they mature.

When we first attempt to apply scene writing to our stories, I take it slowly and work step by step with the whole group. I want students to transfer to their daily writing what they learn from skits, story trips, and reading. I approach this task through a number of group activities. In one lesson, I ask students to find an important action or piece of dialogue in one of their stories. They write the reason they chose this event on a Post-it, mark the passage, and discuss their choice in a group share. We end the discussion talking about the possibility of developing events into scenes.

This activity encourages writers to weigh events and articulate why they're important. Most students can do this: Some, like Ricky, extract a critical line of dialogue and know exactly how it functions in the story. Others select a series of events, realizing that events set up or solve the story problem. Still others read a passage but aren't clear how it functions in the story. Some just don't get it. This activity tells me a lot about them: kids who struggle with this will probably struggle with other scene writing exercises. I keep these writers in mind as we continue our explorations.

I use a combination of drawing, peer response, roving teacher conferences, and rewriting to continue our group thinking process. I start by asking students to sort through their daily writing folder and identify an event from a story in progress that they can rewrite into a scene. They mark the place with a Post-it and submit the story to me. At night I review the stories, noting who needs help with event selection. The next day I confer with students before we move further into the activity.

In some conferences, I help writers articulate why they chose an event.

Day 1	Select event
Day 2	Confer with teacher
Day 3	Draw scene
Day 4	Share and revise

FIG. 2–7: Discovering Scenes: A Group Workshop Activity

Steven, for instance, identified two scenes in "Nine Lives" and felt that one needed development but the other did not:

STEVEN: I have two scenes . . . the off-on scene and when the game goes out. I decided to use the off-on scene for the drawing.

Steven read the first scene:

> "Dad! something is wrong with my PlayStation," I yelled as I ran down the stairs. "Dad?" I said to the air. "In the den," he responded. I walked into the den and almost tripped on a box. My dad was bent over the computer. "Let me guess, the monitor blew?" "Nine times. It went off, on, off, on, off, on, off, on, off, on, off, on, off, on, off, on, off!"

MS. J: So why do you need to revise this?
STEVEN: I'm not quite sure, but I think it needs a little more development besides my dad just leaning over and working on the computer.
MS. J: What do you mean?
STEVEN: I think my dad needs to say something back after I say it goes off and on. Maybe explain what happened.
MS. J: That makes sense. How does your dad feel in this scene?
STEVEN: He's probably annoyed . . . doesn't want to be bothered.
MS. J: You'll need to figure out a way to show that. Could you read the other scene?

Steven read the second scene:

> "XOOXOXO," I said and tapped the keys of my PlayStation controller. "Jump, dang it, Jump!" I screamed at the screen. I jumped off my bedroom floor and onto my bed just as a hunter (in the game) shot nerve gas at me. I died. "Dang, now I'm going to play 'Sahr Hardny.' " I said to nobody. "The raptor is too hard," I went back to the main screen. Back to the password screen. Share password: 0XOOXOXXXOX. "Hey, why did the screen go black? Oh, there, it's back. It happened again!" I said talking to myself.

MS. J: Do you think this scene needs development, too?
STEVEN: This is actually just fine because it's an excellent scene that says that it blacks out and goes back on. Then it's me talking to myself about going back to my password screen.
MS. J: What makes the scene "excellent"?

STEVEN: Well, I showed like when you hear sounds and some dialogue. I think it's good because you can see me playing the game.

I could tell from Steven's response that he understood basic scene elements. He explained what made one scene "excellent" and the other in need of "development." As I asked questions to uncover his reasoning he argued that the successful scene "shows" the story because he used "sounds" and "dialogue" and the reader "sees" him "playing the game."

In other conferences, I help writers identify potential scenes. These students have difficulty weighing events; they see all parts of the story as equally important. I ask them to find the most interesting part of the story, using the same strategy I use when I help writers focus personal narratives. In both dialogues I guide students to work on one event, discussing why it makes a good story or, in this case, a good scene. My conference with Judy went like this:

MS. J: How are you doing? Did you find a part to make into a scene?
JUDY: I don't know which part.
MS. J: Read the story to me and let's figure it out.

Judy reads "The Mystery Cat."

> Michelle sat watching her black cat. Finally their mother said, "Go to bed." Michelle went to bed. She wanted to take the cat to bed but her mom said no. Then she got in bed. Crash! She heard a sound. "What was that sound?" her mom said. Everybody ran downstairs. There was glass all over. There was a big mess. The cat broke the ball. "The China ball broke!" they yelled. The cat ran to the kitchen. She went out the door and they never saw the cat again.

MS. J: Is there a part you like, that you think is really interesting?
JUDY: Well, I like the part where the cat runs away, and I like the part at the beginning. I think I like the beginning one best, where they hear a crash.
MS. J: Why do you like that part?
JUDY: I think it's funny 'cause the cat breaks the China ball.
MS. J: What's a *China ball*?
JUDY: It's this round ball thing. It has colors like brown and yellow. My grandma has one.
MS. J: Do you think you could add to the "crash part?"
JUDY: Yeah, if someone helps me.
MS. J: OK, let's talk about it. Where is Michelle when she hears the crash?
We continued for a few more minutes, discussing details to develop the scene.

It was hard for Judy to isolate events because they seemed equally essential to her. Like most writers, however, she knew what she liked. After discussing her favorite parts of "Mystery Cat," I asked Judy to select the part she liked best. This helped her choose an event to develop into a scene.

I also confer with students to evaluate the need for revision. Mary was in the middle of writing a camping story. In our conference, we discussed whether she needed to rewrite the tent scene.

Mary read her scene:

Suddenly we heard the food supplies going "Bang, crash, clink, clink." I sat up and uncovered the bottom part of my body and peeked through the screen of my tent while scooting toward it on my knees on the covers. And what I saw was a grizzly bear, "Ahhhh!" I covered my mouth quickly and ducked so the bear would not see me, but the sound that the bear was making with the food supplies turned into the sound of footsteps getting softer and softer until I could not hear any more footsteps. So I uncovered my mouth and slowly got under the covers and held my stuffed bear tightly and shut my eyes and slowly feel asleep.

MS. J: Is this a scene?

MARY: I think it is 'cause it shows her in the tent.

MS. J: What do you think about the scene?

MARY: I don't know. I think it might be OK. Maybe needs a little more details.

MS. J: Sounds like you're not sure. Let's look at it carefully and see. What does the little girl do in this scene?

MARY: She uncovers the blanket and looks out and sees the bear.

MS. J: What actions do you show us here?

MARY: Well, she uncovers the bottom part and scoots and looks out of the screen and says, "Ahhhh."

MS. J: So she says something, too?

MARY: She talks to herself.

MS. J: Do you think we can tell how she feels?

MARY: Yah, she's scared when she covers her mouth up and goes back and the bear goes away.

MS. J: There's only one character in this scene, but I think it has lots of details. I picture this scared little girl pulling at her covers, ducking from the bear, lots of good details This scene looks good to me. Let's read your story and see if we can find a part that needs rewriting.

I didn't think Mary needed to revise this scene. She detailed the actions of a scared little girl, showing how her character moves from the sleeping bag to the screen and back to sleep, avoiding an encounter with a bear. I referred to the scene several times as we continued to talk, using it as a standard to evaluate the rest of her story.

After I complete conferences, we fold a large sheet of white paper into four parts. Students write and title the scene in the first square. Then I ask them to close their eyes, visualize the scene, and draw it in another square. During this visualization I encourage them to see new details. When the drawing is complete, they read the first draft and discuss the picture with another student. They ask: How do the characters feel in this scene? They record responses in the third space and rewrite the scene, adding new details, in the fourth. Finally, I ask them to add the revisions to the original story. I circulate around the room conferring with writers throughout these activities.

As students draw I encourage them to picture their scene. Visualization forces them to slow down and think carefully as they pictorially reconstruct setting, characters, and action. Where does my scene take place? Who's in it? What do they look like? What are they doing? How do the characters feel about one another? When does this scene begin and when does it end? In conferences I model these questions, helping writers clarify places, produce new actions, and discover how the scene fits—or doesn't fit—into the story.

A typical drawing conference sounds much like the one I conducted with Olivia just before she drew a scene depicting a fictionalized fight between her and her brother:

MS. J: Tell me about your scene.

OLIVIA: I'm going to draw two stairs right here and me walking down here and my brother is walking down here. We have two stairs.

MS. J: What else do you picture?

OLIVIA: I can't picture anything. I'm sitting right here and my brother is sitting.

MS. J: When you tell us that you gave your brother two black eyes, what happened?

OLIVIA: My brother was the littler one, and I was the bigger one. Then I punched my brother.

MS. J: What did you do when you punched him?

OLIVIA: I just got mad and I pulled his shirt real hard and I punched him. He screamed and started to cry. Then my mom came.

MS. J: How does the other character feel when the little brother cries?

OLIVIA: She's mad. I'm going to put that in.

MS. J: So your scene starts when . . . ?

OLIVIA: When my brother starts to cry.

MS. J: And it ends . . . ?

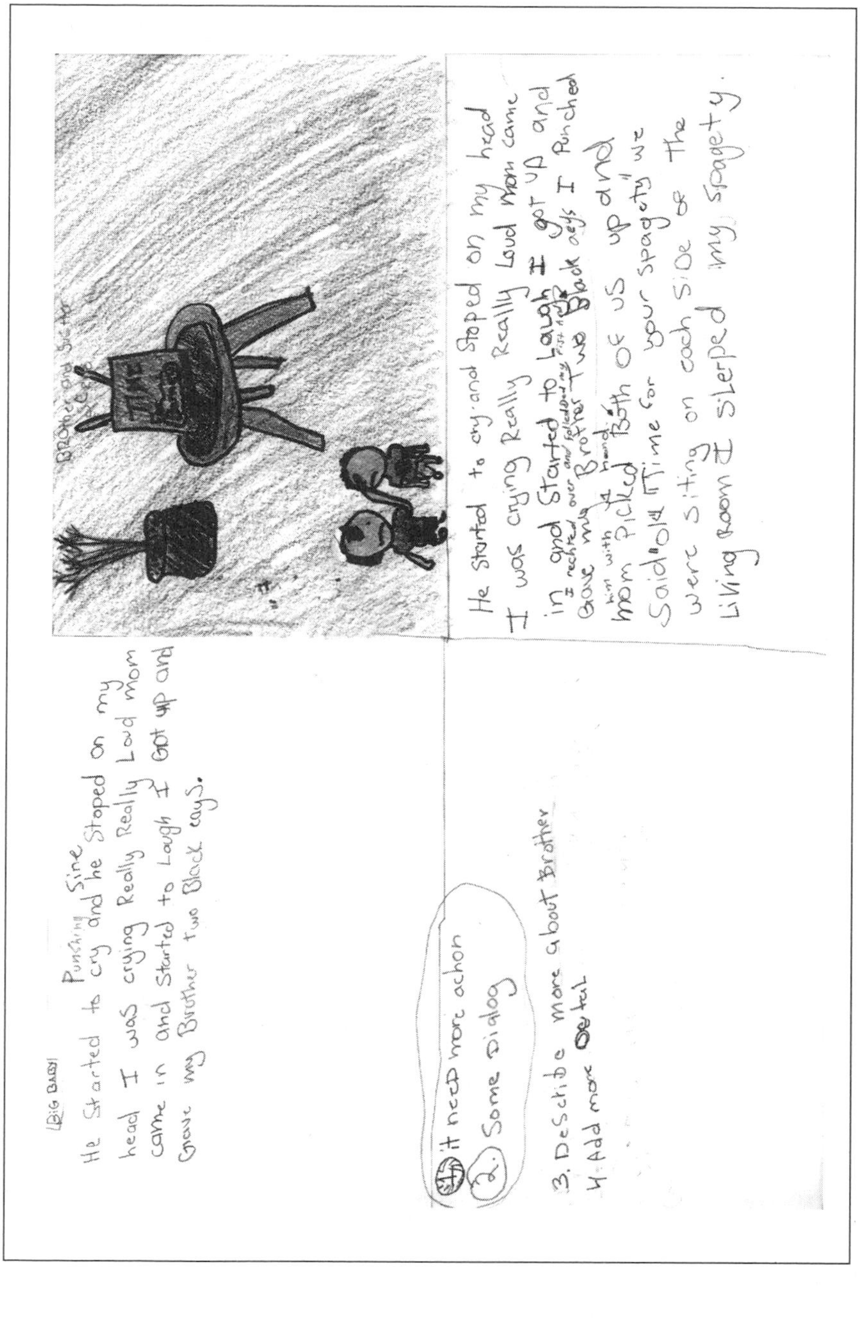

Brother and sister scene

He Started to cry and Stoped on my head I was crying Really Really Loud Mom came in and Started to laugh I got up and Gave my Brother two Black oeys I Punched him with it hand Both of us up and mom Picked Both of us up and Said "oId Time for your spagoty" we were siting on each Side of the Living Room I Slerped my spagety.

BIG BARD

He Started to Punching Sine head I was crying Really Really Loud Mom came in and Started to Laugh I Got up and Gave my Brother two Black eays.

① it need more achon
2. Some Dialog

3. DeScribe more about Brother
4. Add more Detal

FIG. 2–8: Olivia's "Brother and Sister Scene"

OLIVIA: I don't know. It's not done yet.

MS. J: Where does this scene take place?

OLIVIA: In the living room. I can put the TV in because we're watching "Barney." There's a plant and a green rug where we sat.

At first Olivia had difficulty visualizing her scene, but later I watched as she picked up her pencil and drew the characters in the lower right corner of the page. A few minutes later she detailed the *Time for Barney* show she discussed in our talk. Then she added the plant. The next day she told me that she omitted the rug because she forgot it and didn't draw the stairs because "it was too hard to do."

Sometimes drawing conferences take interesting and unpredictable turns. When I talked to Steven just as he finished his "off-on" scene, he wasn't sure the drawing helped him because the picture in his head was much clearer than the one he drew. But he pondered while he worked whether he needed to develop a scene in another piece. I asked him why he thought the drawing made him think of the other story:

> because now I know what a scene is like and where can I put one in "Beer, Beer, Beer." If I do [put in another scene] I know some places, like when I hear the beer bottles click together. My dad runs outside . . . but if I don't put it in, it keeps my story nice and short and on track. Like I thought about, if I put one in, will it keep my story on the focus of my dad running around looking for beers or will it throw my story off? [The new scene] didn't really help. I thought about where I would put it in, about everyone running around trying to find my dad, instead of my dad trying to find the beer.

I circulate from group to group as students read the first draft of the scene and explain their drawing to a peer. Usually I don't intervene in these sessions unless the respondents get stuck and need my help. In the following conversation, Steven explained his drawing and responded to Jacob's questions about the power loss and the box in his scene:

STEVEN: My picture . . . here I am, I tripping over the box. . . . You remember those two bookcases that are near the door in the den. These are two bookcases. This is our futon. This is a window with sun gleaming through. There's my dad with the computer. Here's the monitor of the computer. This is a desk that holds it up. . . . [long pause] Any suggestions?

JACOB: Is your dad mad?

a lives, off, on, scene

off, on scene

"Dad! SOmething is wrong with my playstation," I
yelled as I ran down the stairs. "Dad?" I said to the
air. "In the Den," He respond, I walked into the
Den and almost triped on a box. My Dad was bent
over the computer. *The Mon* "let me guess? the
monter blew," I said. "9 times. It went, off, on, off, on, off,
off, on, OFF, on, off, on, off, on, off, on, off!"

I walked into the Den and almost tripped on
the moniter. My Dad was bent over the old moniter
"let me guess, the Montier blew!" I said. "It must have been
a fuse!" Dad said. "That Explain the playstation!" I mumbled
"9 times! It went on, off, on, off, Etc."

why did it blow?
why Box?
why Did plastation shut Down

FIG. 2–9: *Steven's "Off, On" Scene*

STEVEN: I don't know. I just want him to help. My dad's busy and probably
gets annoyed with me.

JACOB: Is that [computer] going off nine times or more?

STEVEN: Yeah . . . off, on, off, on.

JACOB: Why did it blow? Did you overload it?

STEVEN: It stays on a little longer, and then it went "pouf."

JACOB: Well, why is there a box right here?

STEVEN: The box holds my dad's old fourteen-inch monitor. And he drags it
out just in case something happens to the monitor.

JACOB: Why did you go downstairs?

STEVEN: Well, this is the scene, right there, but to make it make sense you
have to add on the other scene that's on top of it. [read the previous scene]

JACOB: Did you turn off the power or something?

STEVEN: Well, there was something wrong with the PlayStation.

JACOB: That wouldn't make it go off and on like that. It could be a fuse or
something.

After discussing the characters' feelings, Jacob focused Steven's attention on the power problem because he was confused about why the PlayStation went out. He offered a solution, suggesting that Steven expand the scene and explain that the monitor went out because of "a fuse or something."

Steven and Jacob did fine, but I joined Patrick and Ronnie's share after listening to them struggle for several minutes while Patrick explained his drawing:

MS. J: How are you doing, boys? Did you come up with some ideas?
RONNIE: Not yet . . .
MS. J: What's in Patrick's drawing that's not in his story?
PATRICK: The TV. I could change the TV to something else?
MS. J: What do you mean?
PATRICK: To a program.
MS. J: You could. When did you think of the TV idea?
PATRICK: When I drew it. I was thinking I could add that.
MS. J: Ronnie, what else could he put in this scene?
RONNIE: About his sister and the hair dryer?
MS. J: What can you ask him about that part?
RONNIE: Maybe where they were?
MS. J: Sure, and how about asking how Patrick feels about his sister in this scene?
PATRICK: She's annoying. She's always making noises with the hair dryer.

I tried to redirect the conversation to help Ronnie and Patrick think about the characters in Patrick's scene. I left them, and a few minutes later they turned to Ronnie's "Calvin and Hobbes" story, focusing primarily on the details in Ronnie's drawing:

PATRICK: Why is the lamp, like, over the table?
RONNIE: It's just over the table. It's greenish, a green yellow.
PATRICK: And where's Hobbes?
RONNIE: He's upstairs yelling down.
PATRICK: What the heck is that?
RONNIE: That's a light, that's a coat hanger. Did you say why was there a coat on the light?
PATRICK: Yeah, why would there be a coat on the light? Wouldn't it burn your shirt?
RONNIE: No, 'cause it's like further [sic] down. And he doesn't let it hang on the light twenty-four hours a day.

My brief intervention helped Ronnie and Patrick focus during the second half of the share. Patrick's questions allowed Ronnie to explain the

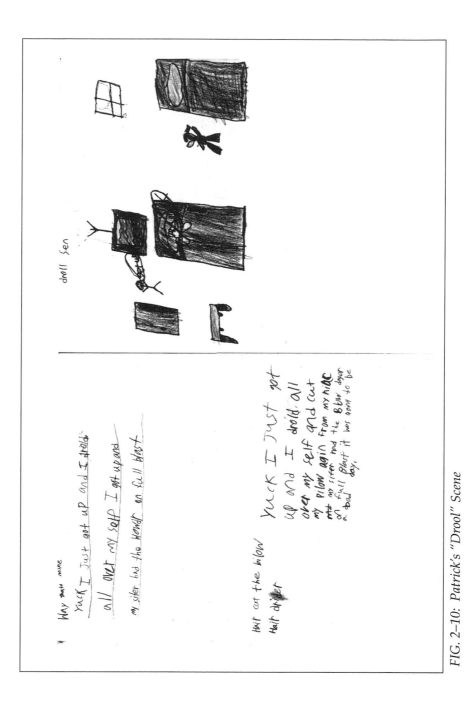

FIG. 2–10: *Patrick's "Drool" Scene*

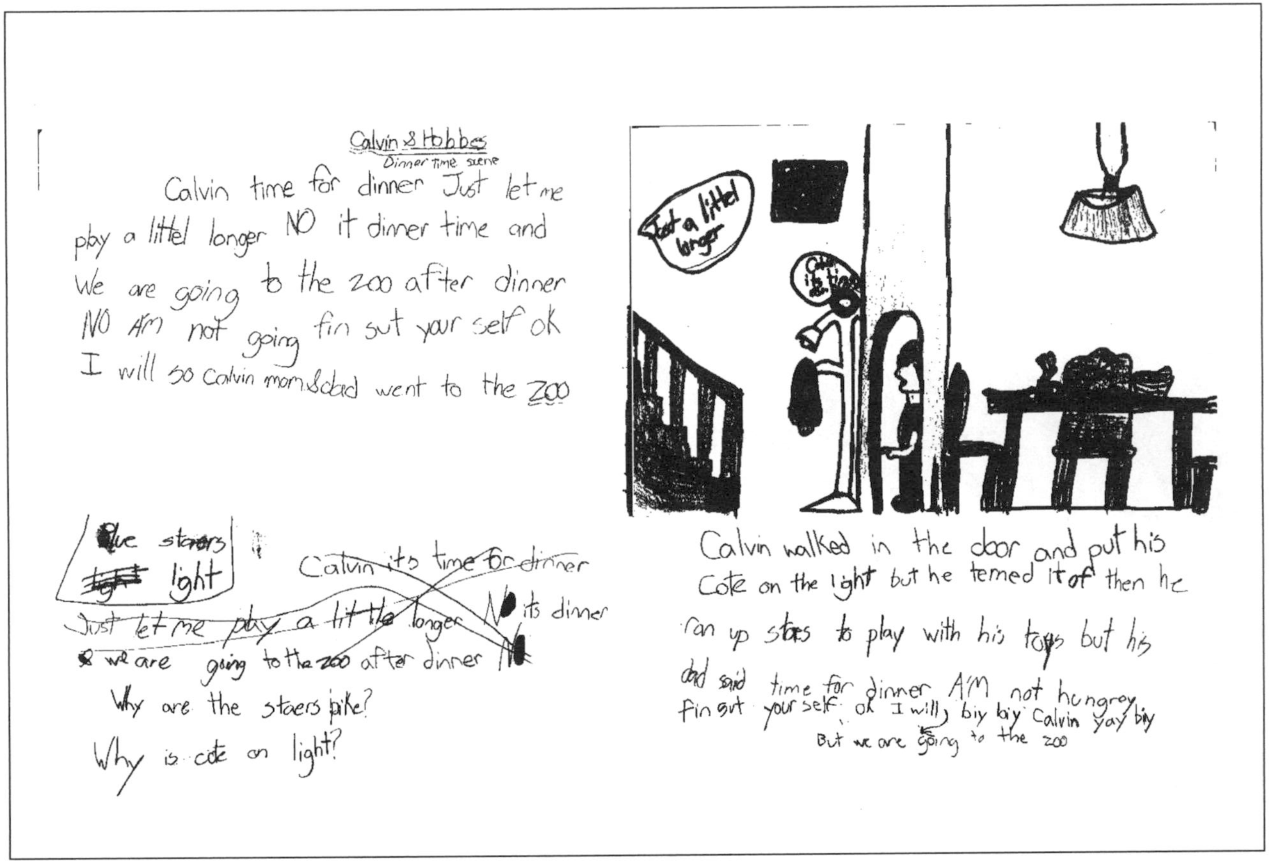

FIG. 2–11: Ronnie's "Dinner Time" Scene

whereabouts of one of the characters and ponder the logic of hanging a coat on a "light that's a coat hanger."

I continue to confer as students rewrite the scene. By this phase of the activity, more mature writers, like Sandy, need little assistance. She shared her scene with Azar, who suggested she show "action from the other team." Sandy told me she thought about the idea of including Julie's thoughts while talking to Azar. She also decided to include the dialogue she sketched into her drawing. In her second draft (changes underlined) she clarified the relationship between her characters:

First Draft of "It's All Up to Me" Scene

There were not many shots in the fourth quarter because of the good defense on both ends. Julie was at the three-point line with the ball with five seconds left on the clock. "Shoot it! Shoot it!" the team yelled. Julie pushed the ball up as hard as she could. It went up and around and around the rim. All of a sudden it popped in. "Yah, we won!" everyone cheered.

Revised Draft

There were not many shots in the fourth quarter because of the good defense on both ends. Julie was at the three-point line with the ball with five seconds left on the clock. "Shoot it! Shoot it!" the team yelled. "It's all up to me. I have to make it." She closed her eyes and pushed the ball up as hard as she could. "Please go in," she thought. It went up and around and around the rim. All of a sudden it popped in. "Nooo!" someone yelled putting her hands in the air. "Noooo!" she yelled again as the ball went in the basket. "Yah, we won!" everyone cheered.

Occasionally students rethink the entire story and delete a scene that no longer makes sense. After his share with Steven, Jacob deleted the "bee scene" and added a new one:

First Draft of "Bee" Scene

Paulo said, "Bee!" I jumped and dropped my controller on the grass and ran in [a] circle yelling, "Ahh, bee, bee, bee . . . !" My motorcycle fell in the middle of the street.

Revised Draft

I heard my motorcycle make a weird sound. "Oh, no, "I've heard that sound before." It was my car battery. My motorcycle fell over.

<u>"No!" I yelled, kicking the dirt. Paulo smiled and ran over my mo-
torcycle. "Why did you do that?" I said. "Because," he said.</u>

Jacob told me that the new scene made more sense for a number of
reasons:

> Once I looked at it with a different view, it didn't make sense. The
> picture helped a little because I saw how it would be and . . . like it's
> a better image than in my head because you could see it. Then I did-
> n't like the bee idea because it didn't make sense 'cause Paulo was
> trying to trick me to drop the controller by yelling "bee." But maybe
> a bee wasn't there. . . . like it was too hard to explain why the bee
> was there just then when Paulo wanted to trick me.

Jacob and Sandy integrated new ideas into their second drafts. Less experienced writers, like Ronnie, however, often replace rather than rethink
the scene. Ronnie's first attempt was almost all dialogue. After his share
with Patrick, he decided to begin the scene with action, using details he had
created in his drawing. He rewrote most of the scene, retaining two short dialogue segments from his first draft:

First Draft of "Dinner Time" Scene

"Calvin, time for dinner." "Just let me play a little longer." "No, it's
dinner time and we are going to the zoo after dinner." "No, I'm not
going." "Fine, suit yourself." "OK, I will." So Calvin's mom and
dad went to the zoo.

Revised Draft

<u>Calvin walked in the door and put his coat on the light—but he
turned it off. Then he ran upstairs to play with his toys, but his dad
said, "Time for dinner." "I'm not hungry."</u> "Fine, suit yourself." "OK,
I will." <u>"But we are going to the zoo. Bye, bye, Calvin." "Yah, bye."</u>

Ronnie, Jacob, and Sandy represent the extremes. Many fifth-graders
simply add a sentence or two of description to a rewrite, usually strengthening the scene in their second draft. James, for instance, took Tony's advice
and added that the first noise in his hallway scene came from a flat tire.

First Draft of "Hallway" Scene

Once again I tiptoed to where the noise came from. When I got to
the hallway, I kneeled down (and) started crawling like an army

man. I felt myself shaking inside. That's how I could tell I was scared. "Boom!" "It's coming from my room," I whispered to myself. I got up and walked in [*sic*] the room where the noise came from. Then I saw nothing.

Revised Draft

Once again I tiptoed to where the noise came from. When I got to the hallway, I kneeled down (and) started crawling like an army man. I felt myself shaking inside. That's how I could tell I was scared. "Boom!" "It came from my room <u>and it sounded like a tire went on [*sic*] flat,"</u> I whispered to myself. I got up and <u>started to walk into the room. I looked through the window. I saw the garbage truck had a flat tire.</u>

Often, drawing and discussing the scene with a peer isn't enough. That's when I step in and talk to students about possible revisions. Marissa's rewrite of the "begging scene" wasn't much better than her original draft.

First Draft of "Begging Aunt Liz" Scene

"Liz, Aunt Liz! Can me and my friends sleep outside?" "I don't know if you could sleep outside." "Please," said Susan. "Okay, fine, tonight is the sleepover."

First Revision

"Liz, Aunt Liz, can me and my friends have a <u>camp out</u>, please? <u>I'll do anything for you.</u>" <u>Susan was begging so much that Aunt Liz said, "Yes, the camp out is tonight." "Thank you, Aunt Liz."</u>

Our rewrite conference focused on the relationship between Marissa's characters, exploring how Aunt Liz and Susan felt about each other:

MS. J: Why do you want to write a scene here?
MARISSA: Because it shows Susan begging her aunt to go outside to sleep. I really want the kids to see that the aunt was thinking about it, like she didn't like it—that is was dangerous and that the aunt didn't trust Susan.
MS. J: So you want to show the aunt worrying in this scene because . . .
MARISSA: The aunt doesn't trust her, so when Susan leaves the backyard, it's like she is responsible. . . .
MS. J: Do you show that?
MARISSA: I don't think so, because she says, "Yes."

MS. J: Could you change it?

MARISSA: Well, like in my picture I drew them looking eye to eye 'cause the aunt wants to look and see if she can trust her.

MS. J: Could you put that in?

MARISSA: She could say that they looked eye to eye and then, "I don't know, Susan, if you could sleep outside."

MS. J: You could show us through dialogue. How about actions?

MARISSA: Aunt Liz could bit her nails.

I tried to encourage Marissa to "get inside" her two characters in this conference. As we talked she realized she already had drawn what she wanted to write and had little difficulty figuring out new dialogue. Marissa revised the scene again, this time hinting at the tension she wanted to show between her characters.

Second Revision

"Liz, Aunt Liz, can me and my friends have a <u>camp out</u>, please? <u>I'll do anything for you.</u>" "I don't know," she said. <u>Liz was biting her lip looking eye to eye at Susan.</u> "Can I, can I?" said Susan. <u>Aunt Liz didn't really trust her.</u> "Okay," said Aunt Liz <u>biting her lip again,</u> "you could." "Cool," Susan said.

This was Marissa's first attempt at writing a scene for a story in progress. She decided where the scene went and practiced how to construct it, but it would take many attempts before she could do this completely on her own. Marissa and other writers need to practice scene writing throughout the year, struggling to create small, focused dramas to bring their stories to life.

Thus, after weeks of skits, story trips, critical reading, and first attempts, scenes—and the actors that create them—become the subject of endless conferences and lessons in our fiction workshop. Shortly after our last story trip, I foreshadow subsequent lessons on characterization by modeling how I write scenes for my own pieces. One year, I gave a series of lessons demonstrating how I developed scenes for "What Did You Say?" a piece about two girls exploring a suspicious noise coming from an upstairs bedroom. This was my first lesson:

I want to revise a part of my piece, today. I'll read it to you. [I read the scene from an overhead transparency]:

Susan quickly brought Linda inside and told her about the sound. They walked toward the stairs.

I think I tell the story too fast here. This is the first time the girls investigate the noise, and I don't think I show how scared they are. I just say that Linda comes inside, and Susan tells her about the sound, and then they walk toward the stairs. I don't picture anything when I read "Susan quickly brought Linda inside." If I describe the hallway the way Linda and Susan see it and make the girls talk to each other, I think I can show *scared* better. I'm going to cross this out and write a scene instead. [I crossed out sentences.]

I'll put myself in Susan's place and see out of her eyes and try to hear what she hears when she approaches the door to let Linda into the house. I picture a small window next to the door, sort of like the windows in my house. At home, I look out the window if I'm not sure who's at the door, and I can imagine Susan doing this. However, I picture a porch that's a lot darker than mine, and I see a small dim light. I'll start the scene showing Susan looking out the window:

> Susan's finger pulled the corner of the curtain open just a sliver. She couldn't see anything. It was dark and quiet on the porch, so she turned the knob slowly, and a quick gush of icy wind rushed through the crack. . . . Seeing Linda's face in the dim porch light, she grabbed her arm and pulled her into the hallway.

I think showing Susan move the curtain to peek out the window shows how cautious she feels. When she turns the knob and sees Linda's face in the dim light, I think the reader can see it, too. This creates a clearer, scarier picture of the action here. I like the phrase "grabbed her arm and pulled her" better than "brought her." "Grabbing and pulling" sounds like she's scared and in a hurry.

I want to put in a conversation next. The dialogue needs to show that they're frightened.

I added to the transparency:

> "Wha . . ."
>
> "Shhh!" Susan's hand slipped over Linda mouth, forcing Linda to step back farther into the darkened hallway. Both girls stood, silent, first staring at each other and then upward toward the stairway leading to the back of the house.
>
> "I heard it again . . . just before you knocked," she whispered.
>
> "I don't want to go up there. . . ."
>
> "Keep your voice down."
>
> "You're not thinking about . . . ?"
>
> "Just follow. . . ."

"Susan!"
"Shhhh. . . ."

I like this conversation. I think "Shhh" shows the reader that Susan's afraid someone's going to hear them. I tried to show that Linda is more frightened than Susan by having her say that she doesn't want to go up the stairs. This fits Linda's personality because Susan's braver than Linda. Maybe I need to add a little more to show just how scared Linda is. [I added this sentence after "into the darkened hallway."]:

Linda's hand trembled as she reached behind to steady herself against the wall.

I began the lesson by explaining why I wanted to change "Susan quickly brought Linda inside and told her about the sound" into a scene. I analyzed the action first, turning to the dialogue in the second part of the discussion. Before I composed the text, I explained how I pictured the scene, seeing through Susan's eyes as she looked out the window. I described how my characters move and talk and then revised the ending to underscore Linda's fearful feelings.

In follow-up student–teacher conferences, we look for places in student stories where characters act out important events, evaluating whether these dramas need more dialogue, movement, or other detail. I ask writers who like to draw to sketch the scene before we talk; others fold paper into four boxes and write what the characters see, hear, touch, and feel. Paulo did this before we discussed how he could turn "Paulo and Patrick walked into the store to buy stuff for Halloween" in "Haunted Night I" into a scene detailing two excited boys naively buying "haunted costumes." We wrote several ideas on a Post-it before Paulo returned to his table to revise the story.

When Lori shared "Dodgeball Can Be Fun But It Can Also Be Evil," we read through the first part of it, looking for scenes. She identified several, including the lead where she introduces the characters and a scene further on that she thought needed revision:

LORI: I found some scenes. The one here . . . on page five . . . I think needs more.
MS. J: Why don't you read it to me?

Lori read the scene:

All the girls gasped when they went into the toy store that looked like kid's heaven with toys of all kinds. For a few minutes the girls just stood there looking at the toys and wishing they lived there. Finally, Cindy said, "Come on, we didn't come here to look at toys. Let's split up and look for dodgeballs. If we don't split up, we'll never find it [*sic*]. This place is as big as a castle." All the girls split up. They didn't notice that someone was following them.

MS. J: What do you think it needs?

LORI: Some more action and a little bit more detail.

MS. J: What kind of action?

LORI: Like Cindy could sort of, like, grab a doll or a toy or something and say, "I've wanted this since I was a little girl."

MS. J: How would that make your scene better?

LORI: It would show more about how they acted in the store.

MS. J: Why do you need to do that?

LORI: This is an important part of the story because it's the part where I give the first clue that somebody wants to kill them.

I jotted down "Add action to the toy store scene" to help Lori remember our conversation. This is all she needs, but Paulo and many others require more. Scene writing is difficult work, demanding a careful examination of the way we write stories. Our initial exploration of scenes draws attention to the importance of *getting inside* a piece, entering a lively make-believe world to allow characters to create the story, but we'll need to revisit the complex craft of scene writing throughout the year before these young authors can add this technique to their fiction writing repertoire.

NOTE

1. For further discussions of scene writing, see Philip K. Jason and Allan Lefcowitz's *Creative Writer's Handbook* (1990, 204–25) and Rebecca Rule and Susan Wheeler's *Creating the Story* (1993, 12–44).

3

Observing Like a Writer

> **Good Writers Know**
> Characters are people who look unique and dress differently.
> Characters are people who move.
> Characters are people who hesitate, interrupt, and gesture
> when they talk.
> Characters are people whose movement and talking reveal feelings.

WHERE WRITERS BEGIN

"Oh, Lori, can you get the door for me?" Ms. J said as she wrote with marker on the [overhead] projector. A tall man walked in with a big box. His walkie-talkie started talking, and as he was talking, the box fell and knocked Marissa out of her chair. "Watch it, fool," Marissa was about to say, but Ms. J was coming toward her. She winked at the tall man as she took the box off Marissa's desk. She opened one end of the box as the tall man walked out of the class. Ms. Jorgensen stopped looking in it and told the class they got a brand new map. Ms. Jorgensen took them out for an early recess, so Ms. J could put the map on the wall.

The lead to Susan's "What Are They Doing to the School Maps?" establishes the conspiratorial tone for her horror/fantasy set in our classroom.

In the story, the teacher and the janitor kidnap children and conspire to extort ransom from their parents. The children magically "enter" the map during a geography lesson and eventually die in various parts of the world. Susan peoples her piece with classmates, friends, relatives, and characters from the movies *Titanic* and *Honey, I Shrunk the Kids*. She chooses these individuals much like a director auditions and selects actors to perform a play, matching real-life personalities with the traits of people who inhabit her fictional world. Smart kids play smart characters; strong kids play strong characters. Each character serves a specific function in the plot, moving the action along through his or her unique attributes and skills. During a conference Susan referred to a list in the margin of her first draft showing where each character enters the map.

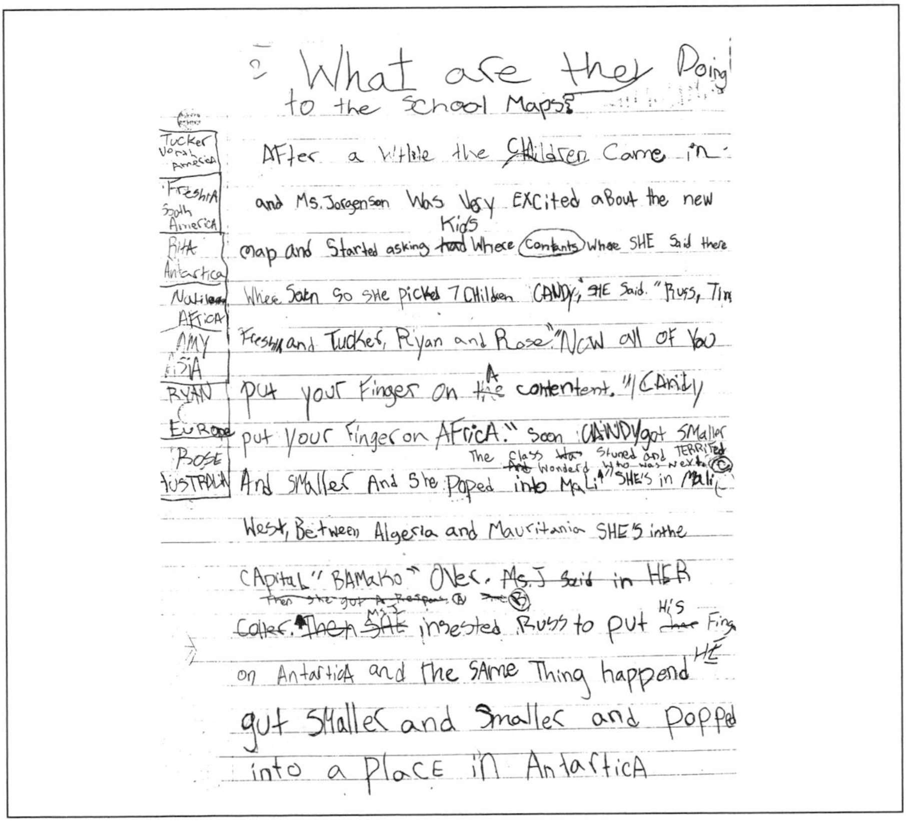

What are they Doing to the School Maps?

Tucker North America | Freshia South America | Rita Antartica | Natilee Africa | Amy Asia | Ryan Europe | Rose Australia

After a while the children came in and Ms. Jorgenson was very excited about the new map and started asking kids where Contants where. SHE said there where seven so SHE picked 7 children. CANDY, SHE said. "Russ, Tim, Freshia and Tucker, Ryan and Rose." "Now all of You put your finger on a contentent." "Candy put your finger on AFRICA." Soon CANDY got smaller and smaller and she poped into Mali. The class stured and TERRIFied wonderd who was next. "SHE'S in Mali West, Between Algeria and Mauritania SHE'S in the Capital "BAMAKO" Over. Ms.J said in HER Coller. Ms.J insested Russ to put his finger on Antartica and the same thing happend he got smaller and smaller and popped into a place in Antartica

FIG.3–1: *Susan's Character Scheme*

MS. J: How did you choose who goes where in your story?

SUSAN: Well, every place suits their [*sic*] personality.

MS. J: So how does Antarctica suit Lori's personality?

SUSAN: Oops, Lori's not going. It's Ross.

MS. J: Who's Ross?

SUSAN: A person on TV in the movie *Honey, I Shrunk the Kids*. Ross is the brother who hit the ball in the window.

MS. J: How does his personality suit Antarctica?

SUSAN: First, I thought about the name. See, he doesn't care about anything. I thought that Lori would freeze to death and then she couldn't help later in the story. But Ross, I put Ross [there] because he is stupid. Well, Lori might actually *think* about how to get warm because she is smart. Cindy and Lori, before they were going to go to the places and die, but now they are just going to help me because they are smart. They can help me figure out who "TM" is and "Roboto."

MS. J: What about Candy? Why did you want her to go to Africa?

SUSAN: She's my sister's friend. I don't think she would survive in Africa. If she was in one of the jungles or something and if she saw poison ivy— she's just not too bright—she'd probably sit in it.

MS. J: And Tim, what about him?

SUSAN: He's my uncle. He's always sick , and he's blind in one eye. I thought I could put him in China. He would die there because there are too many diseases.

Susan planned her selections before writing. She drew a map of the classroom showing the library, the writing center, mailboxes, tables, computers, and desks. She labeled desks with names and used this diagram to select her cast of characters. As she discovered the plot, she revised roles according to an elaborate and thoughtful scheme.

> I changed the people who went in the map so that they could be in the other part of the story because I need them. Lori and Cindy have to save the kids because they are smart, and I need them to help me. Then, like, Marissa and Judy are going to be like body-guards because they are strong. Azar is the only one from the class who's going to go into the map now. Then there's Candy and Ross, Tim, Tucker, Ryan, and Rose. Tucker is my cousin, Ryan's my sister's friend. Candy is my sister-in-law's friend. I put her in because she's not too bright. Rose, I don't know. I just like the name. She's sort of like the girl in *Titanic* but I imagine her smaller, a little younger. I wanted a person that was fancy ... well, she's rich. That's why she's on the *Titanic*. She's sort of a snobby person. She's

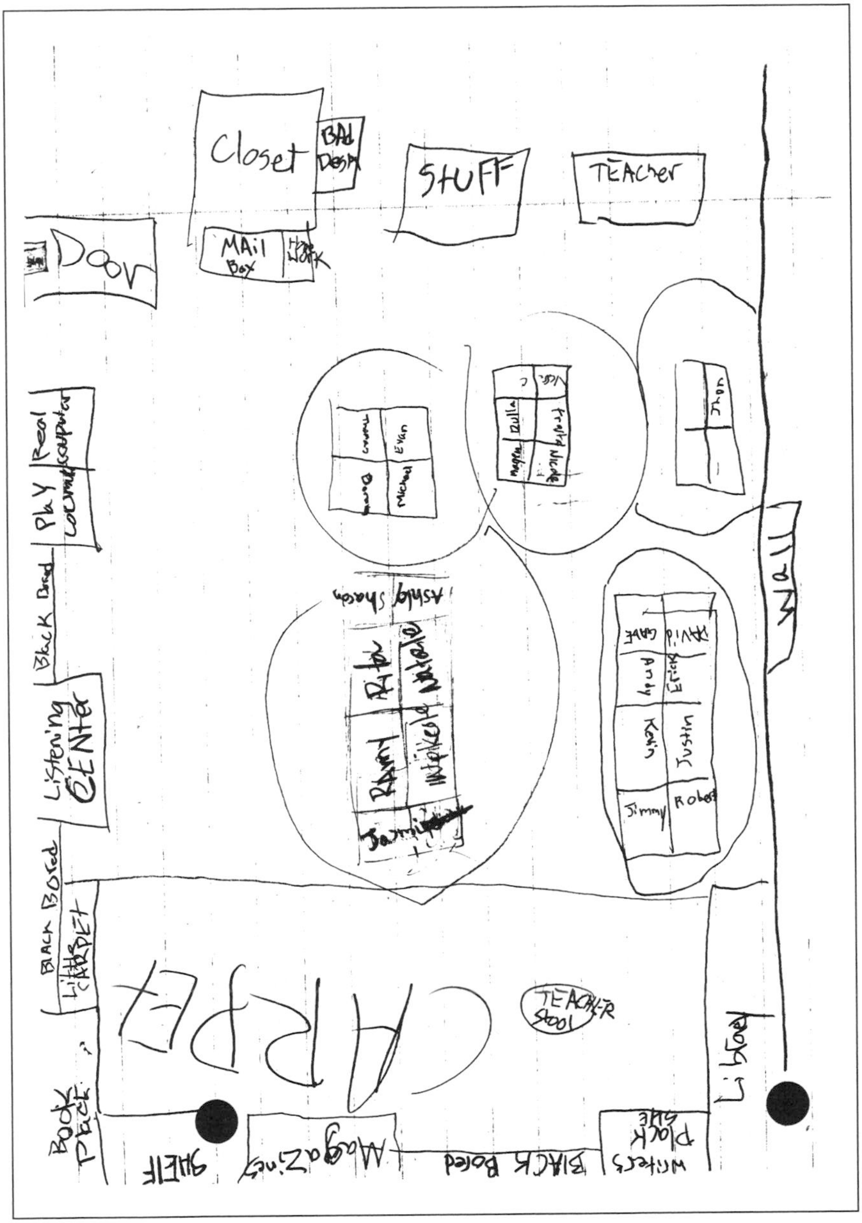

FIG. 3–2: Susan's Map of the Classroom

going into the map. You don't really hear about her. I just like the way she looked. And you're in the story, too. Ms. J looks just like you. She has your glasses, too. The Tall Man, he's the janitor at our school. I'm scared of the janitor. He's weird. He reminds me of Lori's mom's boyfriend.

Although Lori and Candy in Susan's story act exactly like Lori and Candy in real life, young writers sometimes move away from this one-to-one relationship, crafting truly fictionalized characters, new personalities synthesized from the people they know. In this sense, these young authors mimic their adult counterparts, drawing inspiration for characters "somewhere between life and pure fantasy" (Burroway 2000, 95). In "Lip Gloss," Sandy created two synthesized characters. She pictured one better than the other.

Sandy read her story:

"Jenny, stop playing with that lip gloss," Jessica snapped.

"She's just showing off. She's probably going to make a story about it, Michelle whispered.

"Hey, that's a good idea, Michelle," Jenny said.

"Jenny, you're so annoying. I'd rather sit next to a boy than you," Michelle said.

Jenny got up to get another sheet of paper. As she walked over, her brown, ugly-colored bell bottoms shined in the light.

"Jenny is such a nerd. I was just kidding about her story," Michelle said to Jessica.

"Whatever," Jessica replied.

Jenny worked on the lip gloss story for over two weeks. The last thing she needed was a share. She picked Jessica, Beth, and Olivia. The three bells rang and partner share was over.

"Hey, great story, Jenny," Beth said.

"Yeah, it was great," Jasmine and Olivia said. As Jenny walked back to her seat, her long brown hair that was in a lop bun swung side to side.

"How much did it suck?" Michelle asked.

"Actually, it was really good," said Jessica, "What do you have against Jenny, anyway?"

"She's always in my face and certain little things bother me like when she sticks her tongue out at people and the way she rolls her eyes. It's just annoying," Michelle explained."And how can Jenny's stories ever be any good?"

"Just wait until Author's Celebration, you'll see," Jessica shouted.

"Everyone come to the rug. It's time for Jenny's celebration," Ms. J. called. Everyone ran to the rug. Jenny pulled out her chair. She took tiny little baby steps so she could waste time because you could tell she didn't want to read her story in front of Michelle. She looked like she was a red balloon she was blushing so much. Everyone could tell that Jenny was nervous. She really wanted Michelle to like her story, but if Melissa said she liked it, Jenny would think Melissa liked her, which would be really bad for Michelle. Jenny went on with her story. When she was finished, people said what they liked. Then they all went back to their seats.

"Did you like the story, Michelle?" Jessica asked.

"Yeah, it was OK," she said.

"You liked my story? YES!" Jenny shouted, jumping up and down with joy.

"Hey, that doesn't mean I like you, show-off!" Michelle said.

"I'm so glad you liked my story. So you want to play with me at recess?" Jenny said.

"Please, someone tell me why did I do this to myself? GET OUT OF MY FACE!"

MS. J: I notice in your story that you use Jessica's, Olivia's, and Michelle's names for your characters. You call one character "Jenny." We don't have a Jenny in our room. Is this character based on someone you know?

SANDY: Jenny is Beth. I decided not to use her name because she might not like what the story's about. She said I could [use it] but she didn't know the story.

MS. J: Does Jenny look like Beth?

SANDY: No, I got the idea . . . I used to wear my hair in a bun, so I put that in there. It's from a lot of different people. Like, her face is sort of small like my friend Susan [sic]. She used to live next door at my old house but we moved. And the bell bottoms, I just made those up.

MS. J: Is Jenny like anyone you've ever known?

SANDY: No, not really. But I can picture her. I pictured her when I started writing the story. She's short and likes basketball like me. Her hair's sort of brown.

MS. J: How about Olivia?

SANDY: She has a little part in the story. She's exactly like Olivia, but she doesn't do much.

MS. J: What about the Michelle character? Does she look and act just like Michelle in our class?

SANDY: Well, not exactly, but kind of. Like, no, probably exactly.

MS. J: What about Jessica?

SANDY: No, I pictured Jessica as way different because that's supposed to be me. If I used me, it would be too much like personal narrative. But the story Jessica doesn't really look like me. She's like older than me. They're older characters, kind of. She's got different hair and like different colors. But I don't picture her a lot. She doesn't really act like me, either. She talks different from me, like she'll say different things in different ways. She's just "me" because I was in the story in the first place.

Sandy could have substituted another real-life character for Beth like Susan substituted Ross for Lori. Instead, she constructed Jenny, a fictional character who makes sense in the story. Despite this sophistication, Sandy created Jenny and Jessica for social reasons. She wanted to use Beth in her piece but decided to construct a fictional character because Beth "might not like what the story's about." Sandy disguised herself as Jessica because she didn't want her story to be too much like personal narrative. The social constraints of fifth-grade school culture molded her decisions, not her understanding of the function of characters in narrative writing.

Ten-year-olds rarely plan and execute detailed and self-conscious character schemes like Sandy's and Susan's. If writers articulate a strategy, most adopt the "I do it because I don't have to explain it" approach. As Jacob told me, he used Garfield in his stories "because a lot of kids know Garfield. If I used another character, they'd say, 'Who's that?' It's just easier to do it that way."

Casting classmates and well-known media personae as characters serves two important functions for ten-year-olds. Writers cut to the action when they don't have to explain the people in their stories. Students come to school groomed to create such action-driven fiction after years and years of seeing it on TV, in movies, and in video games. Also, this type of story suits the social-emotional development of the average fifth-grader. Though acute observers in many respects, ten-year-olds often can't describe what they experience at home, on the playground, and in the classroom. The characters they create mirror what they know about the world.

Using friends as characters serves another purpose. Fifth-grade writers use stories to explore and extend social relationships. Susan attended to each prospective actor's personality and social standing as she selected participants for her story. She's the main character, casting her best friend Lori as the student who helps her solve the mystery of the disappearing kids "because Lori's smart, and she likes that character." She chose two popular girls, Olivia and Marissa, to assist them. Azar has few friends at school, and in the story, she dies somewhere in the Sahara Desert. The map fantasy serves Susan's social purposes, echoing her understanding of classroom roles while cultivating friendships with Lori, Marissa, and Olivia. As Dyson

(1997, 12) suggests, authors shape stories according to their "social goals, their need for social belonging, their need to define a place for themselves in a society crisscrossed with difference."

Sandy, Susan, and Jacob believed in their characters: they saw them, heard their voices, knew how they should act. They thoughtfully selected them from scores of people they know. Once selected, characters aren't just actors playing roles; they coauthor the piece. On some subtle level Susan and Sandy take the real Lori, the flesh-and-blood Olivia into account as they discover the story. After all, Lori and Olivia are classmates, and the girls share ideas with them as they write. They want Lori and Olivia to like their pieces, to approve of the roles they play in their complex, classroom-based tales. Likewise, Jacob molds his story to conform to the Garfield he knows from countless days of TV watching and perusing Garfield books.

What is striking about these plot-driven stories is that the authors reveal so little about their characters. We don't see the real Cindy's scuffed sneakers and uneven shoestrings or watch the way Lori tilts her head to one side when she's explaining something or hear Olivia's infectious giggle when she's caught off guard. We never learn that Sandy's Jenny likes basketball or sports a tight brown bun on the back of her head. Jacob tells us little about Garfield's distinctive stripes or his sassy relationship with his owner, Jon. Nor do we sense how these characters feel or what motivates their actions. Jacob, Susan, and Sandy know these characters well but keep them shadows in their respective fictional worlds. The authors understand the characters they create but lack the skill and desire to bring them to life in the pages of their stories.

Jacob, Susan, and Sandy's writing underscores an important observation about the way kids construct characters: Young writers base characters on friends, family, and media personas but hardly ever show us how these characters talk, move, and feel. Writers imply personality through the role the character plays in the story. Personal nuance remains subjugated to the push and pull of the plot.

This fundamental understanding—that kids know but don't show characters—informs the way I teach characterization. My primary task is not to help students create characters but to guide them to discover what they already know, to see the *real* people behind their fictional actors. There's really nothing new about this: mature writers are acute observers of people; young writers can learn to do this, too. Thus, we begin our rethinking by learning to observe like writers, discovering how classmates, family, and friends dress, move, and talk, and by discussing what these observations reveal about the internal world of thought and feeling. In a sense, this process takes us inside the scene, focusing our attention on the people writers use to drive the drama. We employ our senses again, opening our eyes, listening, and studying what Burroway (2000, 12) calls "the indirect methods of character presentation." In each exercise, we observe, write, analyze excerpts from books, and evaluate how we employ—or don't employ—a given method of presentation in our stories.

THE WAY PEOPLE LOOK

I begin our study of characters with an examination of the way people look. I start with appearance because it's concrete and easily observed. Ten-year-olds spontaneously write about hair color and age but use appearance details mechanically, throwing them into the text without understanding how they affect the reader's perceptions. Phrases like "the blond boy" or "she was twelve years old" tell us little about motivation and personality. Good writing reveals uniqueness, individual qualities we can identify in a crowd. My goal is to teach writers to turn routine descriptions into, as Christopher Leland (1998, 171) suggests, details of dress and body that "reveal something, cue us as to some larger element of the character's self."

We use our Thinking About Fiction notebooks to record observations about appearance. I begin by asking students to write one thing about their appearance that distinguishes them from others in the class. Then they do the same for a classmate and share observations in a writers' circle where we discuss whether the attribute reveals uniqueness. The process is fun and simple: a student reads a characteristic, and we guess whom it describes. Students who identify others by "long brown hair" or "white sneakers" soon discover that fifteen kids can be described the same way. Writers who use unique descriptors learn that their words identify a single individual. We had no trouble guessing that Jacob was the person who "plays basketball with a broken wrist," Sophia the one who wore "a big fluffy brown jacket to school," or Cindy the kid with "Air tennis shoes, a little velvet jacket, and light-colored nail polish." We close the circle discussing how carefully chosen words and phrases reveal something special about characters, whereas generic terms tell us very little.

We continue our study by discussing excerpts from familiar novels, analyzing how authors use details of dress and physical appearance to create unique and believable characters. In one lesson, we read the lead to *Bridge to Terabithia* and discussed how Katherine Paterson (1977, 1) used clothing to show Jess' passion for running. She told us that Jess "slid out of the bed and into his overalls. He didn't worry about a shirt because once he began running he would be as hot as popping grease even if the morning air was chill, or shoes because the bottoms of his feet were by now as tough as his worn-out sneakers." We discussed Paterson's descriptive phrases and ended by sharing how we pictured Jess as he jumped out of bed and headed barefoot to his morning workout.

In another lesson, we read through our daily writing, looking for ways we use appearance in our stories. Except for an occasional "red-eyed vampire" or monster with "blood dripping from his teeth," we usually find little to list on the overhead projector. We discuss our pattern, noting that most writers omit appearance details when they create characters, then we move on to select an interesting character from a story in progress to explore and develop. I ask writers to think about the real-life models for these characters: the classmates, relatives, or movie and book personae they use to create their fictional people. They describe the character to a partner, take notes, and add appearance details to the story. I conduct short conferences helping writers decide how to integrate this new information into the piece. For some, like Ronnie and Tommy, the activity leads to simple revisions. Ronnie had difficulty distinguishing between talking and appearance, adding that Ash in Pokemon World War I "talks about Pokemon" and his "hair sticks up." Tommy's revisions were limited by his model, an illustration of Jack from the book *Jack Jumped over the Candlestick*. Tommy said that Jack has "green pants" and a "red hat."

Other writers make more elaborate changes. Marissa showed Sandy's blond hair, blue eyes, long shirts, and black Nike shoes in her story "First Day of High School." Susan detailed Mary's appearance, adding that the main character in "Wash Up" has "dirty white shoes with two silver lines across [that] she wears everyday [*sic*] with white socks that you can see because she folds her jeans."

Homework provides extra practice, allowing students to observe the appearance of people in another setting. Some respond to this activity by writing one-sentence descriptions. Paulo observed his neighbor and wrote "Josh was running and jogging in his first Air Nike shoes." Others use movements to show subtle detail. Susan described Aunt Patricia blow-drying her "curly salt-and-pepper hair."

> Patricia blew her hair back. All the different curly colors flung every way. Black, white, brown. Then they quickly fell back down causing [her hair] to puff up.

In a similar fashion, Lori sprinkled nail polish and pigtail details into a piece about her big sister sleeping in the backyard (appearance details underlined):

> Mimi looked very sleepy and bored sitting on the grass. Mimi went into her tent and started to fix her sleeping bag. As she unfolded her

sleeping bag her <u>nail polish glistened in the moonlight</u>. She <u>undid her hair and tied it into two pigtails</u> and crawled into her sleeping bag and fell asleep the second her head touched the pillow.

THE WAY PEOPLE MOVE

We study movement next, turning our attention to how people gesture and move their bodies. Young writers rarely give us these details of characterization. They say that characters "get angry" but hardly ever show grimaces, clenched fists, glares, or set jaws. Also, students don't make the distinction between action and movement: in Susan's map fantasy, when Ms. J sent the class to an early recess, her action changed the story; the way a student tripped as she raced out the door "characterizes without moving the plot forward" (Burroway 2000, 108). Kids can't grasp this subtle difference but can learn to see fictional actors the way they see real people, fleshing out personality by showing how characters walk, sit, or exhibit feelings through facial expressions and gesture.

We explore movement the same way we explore appearance, repeating our four-part process: we observe, write, and discuss; we analyze examples from books; we evaluate our stories; and then we practice at home. We start by brainstorming words to describe the way kids move on the playground, listing verbs like "dodge," "tag," "skip," "toss," "slide," "nod," "wave," "leap," and "point." At recess, students choose one person each to observe, identify the playground activity, and for ten minutes record words or short phrases to describe movements, then they write a lead to a story incorporating their observations. In the classroom, we share lists and stories, discussing how words describe particular playground games. Jacob's list led to a discussion of the distinction between football and tag:

MS. J: Jacob, could you read your words?
JACOB: Eat, walk backwards, put hands in pocket, yell, stagger backwards, block, putting hands together to signal, tag, bump, talk, stiff arm, get open, push, charge.
MS. J: Can you tell what activity Jacob was observing?
AZAR: Tag?
MS. J: What words make you think of tag?
AZAR: Tag, run . . .
MS. J: Could these movements describe any other activity?
PAULO: Football?
MS. J: What words sound like football?
PAULO: Like block, run backwards, signal, tag, stiff arm.

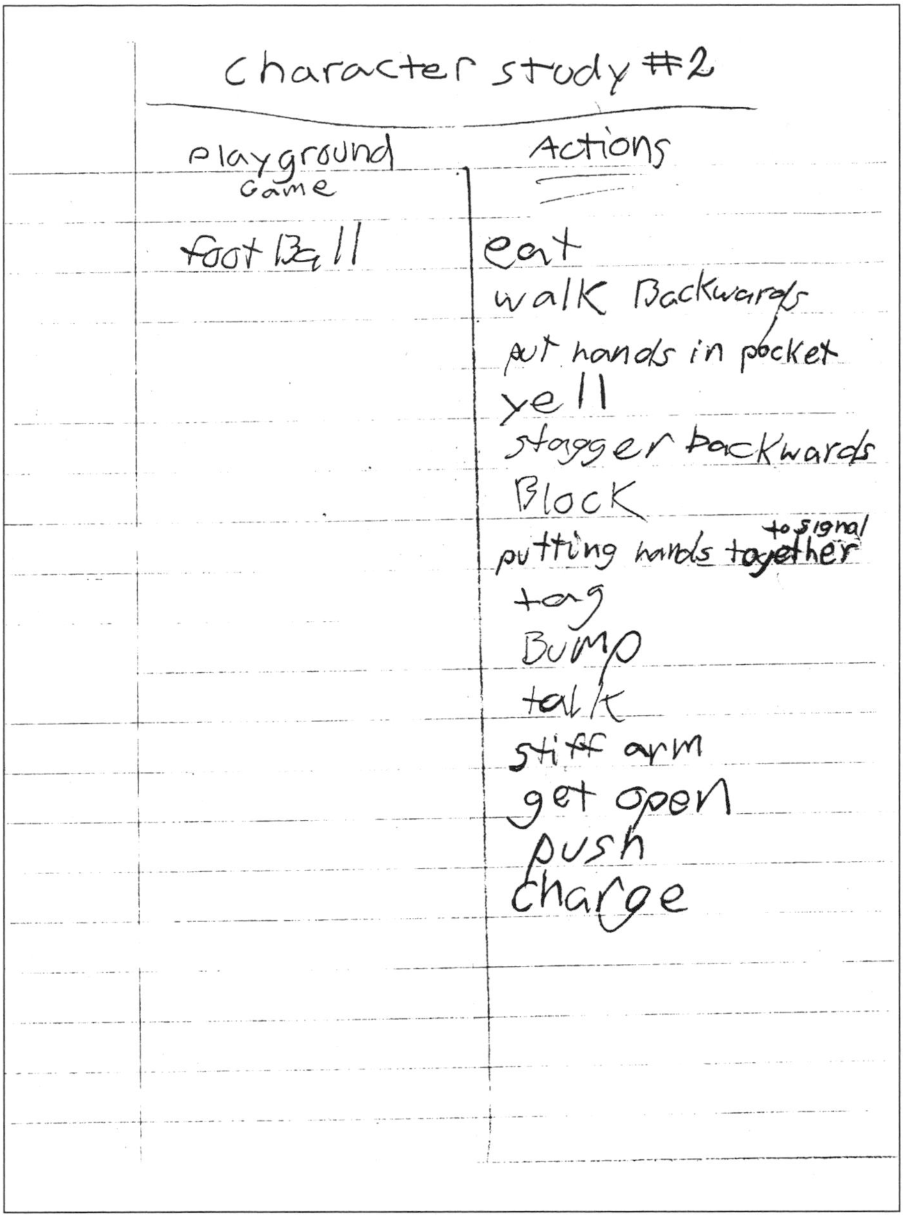

Character study #2

Playground Game	Actions
football	eat
	walk Backwards
	put hands in pocket
	yell
	stagger backwards
	Block
	putting hands together _to signal_
	tag
	Bump
	talk
	stiff arm
	get open
	push
	charge

FIG. 3–3: *Studying Movement on the Playground: Jacob's Notes*

MS. J: Why don't Jacob's words describe tag to you?
CHARLES: 'Cause you don't run backwards or stop.
JIMMY: And "stiff arm" is what you do in football.

We read student stories next, evaluating how writers use words to show movement. Jacob incorporated most of his list (words underlined) into his football piece.

> "Hike!" Alex yelled. Daniel <u>bumped</u> the person that was <u>blocking</u> him. "I'm open!" Daniel screamed to Alex. Alex <u>passed</u> Daniel the ball. Daniel <u>charged</u> someone and <u>blocked</u> the second person but the third person <u>charged</u> Daniel. Daniel <u>staggered backwards</u>. When Daniel <u>staggered backwards</u>, somebody <u>tagged</u> him. Daniel <u>walked</u> back to the line of scrimmage. "Hike!" Alex said again. "I'm open!" Daniel <u>yelled</u>. Alex tried to <u>pass</u> Daniel the ball, but someone on the other team <u>blocked</u> the ball.

Sandy captured the details of a basketball shot by a sixth-grade girl:

> Jennifer <u>jumped</u> up to catch the ball. Her arms and hands went <u>up and down to dribble</u> to the foul line. Her <u>elbows went up and she pushed</u> the ball to the basket, her <u>wrist forward</u> as she shot. "Oh man," she said as her ball hit the rim. Next she tried a backward shot. She <u>lifted her head. [Her arms] went behind her</u> as she looked at the basket. Her arms <u>went up</u> and the ball went to the basket, "Yeah, it went in!" she yelled.

Our observations led to a discussion of how movements show emotion. We talked about how kids feel when they jump to catch a ball or shoot and miss the basket, then we worked in small groups to make up sentences describing actions that show specific feelings. Many students stuck with "mad," "sad," or "happy," but some created scenarios to illustrate other emotions. Paulo and Jacob wrote that Ned was "hurt, embarrassed, angry" when he "tripped and fell in the mud." Mindy and Emily said that "the mean girl" who lost the contest was "disappointed and upset."

It's difficult for ten-year-olds to apply these isolated lessons to daily writing, but I start by reviewing scenes from our reading. In one lesson, I read sections from *Little Giants* by Sheila Black (1994, 8). Students wrote what they observed and then we discussed how the author used phrases like "called out the instructions," "the young players fanned out across the field," and "Butz punted the ball" to show a group of characters moving about on a make-believe football field.

JOHN [big smile]: Why? Come on, it's just for a little while. Your mom won't mind if . . .
CHARLES: I can't. I have to go home.
MS. J: What do you think John was feeling as he was asking Charles to come over?
AZAR: That he was being pushy, would you come over to my house, why not, over and over.
MARISSA: Like, this is my house, and I want you to play.
MS. J: Maybe he was feeling a little frustrated because he had to ask Charles so many times?
CINDY: He had his feelings hurt.
MS. J: He might feel hurt. How about Charles, what do you think he was feeling?
BETH: Like he didn't want to go.
STEVEN: Mad and sad.
MS. J: Why was he mad?
STEVEN: Maybe because he wasn't sure if he wanted to go.
MS. J: So we could say he was feeling a little. . . .
STEVEN: Unsure.

Students struggled to separate behavior from motivation in this discussion, unable to move beyond "mad" and "sad." They retold the dialogue when I asked for underlying intentions. I responded by separating doing from saying and provided words to describe feelings, moving beyond simple categories to resee actors as "frustrated" or "hurt" or "unsure."

We take our observations to the lunch room, next, trying to listen and remember snippets of everyday conversation. Students record what they saw and heard in their fiction notebook when we return to class. Most recall short interchanges, some with amazing detail and insight. Lori listened to Leanora and Tahlei arguing over money, noting that the girls were "singing, stopping in the middle of a sentence, laughing, talking loud and soft, and waving hands and stomping feet." She inferred from the dialogue and body language that the participants were "mad, happy, confused, and worried." Less observant writers still manage to make observations, though some, like Jessica, confuse indirect and direct dialogue, telling us what the character says rather than recording actual speech.

We try one more exercise before observing again. I ask writers to work with a partner and create three quotations, each showing a different emotion. In this lesson, I want to develop vocabulary to describe how people feel when they talk. Again, kids quickly define *sad*, *mad*, and *happy*. Here Susan and Olivia discuss ways to show *anger*:

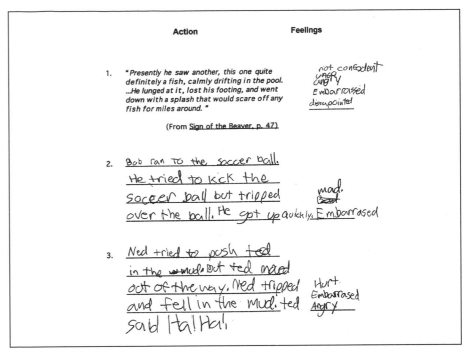

FIG. 3–4: *Writing Actions to Show Feelings*

After discussions like this, I ask writers to review their own stories and identify places where they might add similar descriptions. With a partner they brainstorm revisions while I circulate and help them decide where to add new sentences or insert new words. Usually these revisions improve characterization: Ricky's "Ricky walked up to James" turned into "Buddy dragged Ricky up to James." Jessica's "Ericka showed her cards to Dolly" became "Ericka was sitting on her knees showing her cards to Dolly."

We try the lesson one more time as a home assignment. This sometimes produces relatively simple descriptions like Marissa's "As Roy was playing he was talking, screaming, and running around." Other write-ups sound like personal narrative. Susan observed her older sister, writing:

Nancy took a big bite and chewed quickly to look up at the TV. But only to look down and grab another cracker and then swing her foot toward me, noticing I wrote about her.

But many writers incorporate observations into a storylike form. Lori wrote:

"I'm so bored," Grace said yawning. Grace twisted her head and took a look at the TV controls. She got up and leaned over to reach for the controls. Grace moved her fingers up and down, switching from channel to channel until she found the right channel. "Hurray!" Grace shouted and jumped up and started shaking her butt and dancing around.

THE WAY PEOPLE TALK

Youngsters seem to take an all-or-nothing approach to dialogue, initially telling stories with no talking at all. However, once they discover dialogue, they can't keep quiet. The writer's voice becomes the character's voice: talking goes on and on with little attention to setting or other narrative detail. This voice infuses life into previously boring pieces but—like a radio show without sound effects—produces disembodied characters, placeless worlds. It's difficult to visualize Mustafa's "Fire God" because it's all dialogue:

> "Can we play 'Fire God'?" I said. "John is up." "Hi, Fire God, my name is John. When do I go to the moon? I want to bring jelly and a munchy. Can I go?" "Yes, you can. Tony K., you're next." "When I go to the moon I want to bring a book and some cards to trade. Can I go?" "No, you can't." "Mustafa, our [turn's] up." "Hi, my name is Mustafa. I want to go to the moon. I want to bring some gum and jelly beans. . . ."

A number of other patterns emerge when young writers use dialogue. They confuse everyday talk with fictional talk, filling stories with meaningless chatter, or what Chiarella (1998, 4) calls "jabber." *Jabber* is the "Can I go?" "Yes, you can" interchange between the three boys and the Fire God in Mustafa's story. Mustafa and other young writers also use dialogue as exposition, addressing the reader to explain what's happening in the story. "Hi, my name is" introduces each character, and "you're next" or "your turn's up" informs us that a new petitioner is about to address the Fire God. The boys' fate in this story turns on the will of the god, but the matter-of-fact banter shows little tension or drama. Good dialogue is conversation between characters, "talk for the characters' purposes, not for the benefit of the audience," talk that reveals " the characters' nature, needs, and intentions," showing them "in immediate relation to others" (Jason and Lefcowitz 1990, 288, 195).

Some ten-year-olds skip the loquacious phase and quickly learn to write effective dialogue, seamlessly balanced with action and narration.

Tommy blended these elements in the first draft of "Carrots from Mars," which began like this:

> I looked through my telescope and saw something that looked like a sphere except it was orange. "Ah, Tony, look, an orange comet. It's coming. And boy, you've got to see it. It's big." "Naa-ahh." Tony picked up the bowl of popcorn, took just one last look at the TV, then walked over. He looked in the telescope, then dropped the popcorn. Jacob and Mustafa were jumping on the bed having a pillow fight. Jacob nailed Mustafa in the head. Kapooommm! "Tony, you klutz!" said Jacob finally noticing that Tony dropped the popcorn. Jacob grabbed the chips and walked over.

Tommy used dialogue well, but most kids need coaching. When I teach this, I help writers identify jabber, convert expository dialogue into action or narrative, and write fictional talk that shows feeling and intention. We begin with observations, listening to everyday chit-chat and recording gestures and body language. This activity helps kids understand that real talk is animated and intentional though sometimes filled with meaningless chatter. Two kids role-play a conversation before we attempt to observe *real* talking in the school cafeteria. The group sets up a simple situation, one resembling the skits students perform earlier in the year. Two actors play out the scene while the audience takes notes. This performance provides listening and recording experience even though staged conversation lacks the pacing and give-and-take context of authentic interaction. When we discuss the role play afterward, students usually notice that people hesitate before responding, speak over each other, nod their head and gesture, change tone, and make faces as they talk. We try to connect these dynamics to underlying feelings and intentions. This is a big challenge for young writers. In the following discussion, students debriefed a scene in which John invites a reluctant Charles to play at his house after school.

John and Charles stood in front of the group.

JOHN: Do you want to come over to my house?
CHARLES: I can't.
JOHN: Come on, you can play my PlayStation.
CHARLES: I have to go home after school.
JOHN: Just for a little while?
CHARLES: I can't. I . . .
JOHN: Ask your mom.
CHARLES: I have to go home. [starts to giggle]

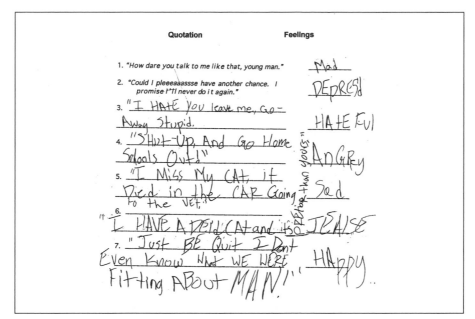

FIG. 3–5: *Writing "Quotations" to Show Feelings*

OLIVIA: Let's be angry. . . .
SUSAN: OK, make it a dialogue. . . .
OLIVIA: She says, "Shut up."
SUSAN: We have to say more, like. . . .
OLIVIA: No, "Shut up, go home, school's out."
SUSAN: Yeah.
OLIVIA: She's mad. . . .
SUSAN: No, angry.

Others, however, ponder less commonplace emotions. Marissa and Olivia discussed whether "She does not look good in that skirt, but I do" shows jealousy or boasting. They decided that the character feels both emotions, separating the sentence into two distinct parts:

MARISSA: Do you think this is "jealous"?
JUDY: Not this part [refers to "but I do."], but that part [points to "She does not look good in that skirt"].
MARISSA: Yeah, I think she's kind of boasting [refers to "but I do"].
JUDY: Like she thinks she's the best. OK, let's write that.
MARISSA: Well, she's jealous, too. I'll put the boasting part.

Often, pairs struggle to separate doing from feeling in this activity. Azar reminded Beth that a person who says "Could I please have another chance? I promise I'll never do it again" can't feel *lying* because "lying is what he does, not like his feelings." When we share in a writers' circle, I look for similar confusions and try to steer students away from the *mad, sad,* and *happy* syndrome. In our discussions, writers read quotations, and the group identifies the feeling. Mary's quotation, "Why do I always get the blame for something he does?" provoked the following responses:

BETH: It sounds like "unhappy."
MS. J: Other words besides "unhappy"?
RICKY: Disappointed.
TONY: Blameful.
OLIVIA: Angry.
JACOB: Jealous.
MS. J: Maybe feeling all of those thing? Mary, what did you say?
MARY: Curious.
MS. J: Why?
MARY: Because he wants to know why his parents blamed him.

These discussions help writers identify intention when we observe dialogue again, this time on the playground during recess. Many students continue to describe emotions as "mad" and "happy" but now add descriptors like "embarrassed," "mischievous," and "curious." Susan, for instance, overheard two girls teasing each other about clothes, characterizing them as "loud and excited." Others described kids as "jumpy," " silly," and "funny." I see similar responses when students record dialogue at home. Lori said her sister felt "disgust" when she said "Eww, a spider!" Marissa documented a conversation between two friends, noting that "Ysenia is feeling bad and nervous. Jenny is not understanding what Ysenia is trying to say."

Next we discuss the role dialogue plays in fiction, noting that people in stories don't always talk like people in real life. Writers create dialogue to reveal characters, leaving out everyday banter. We contrast the jabber, incomplete sentences, and false starts we hear on the playground with dialogue from scenes in well-crafted novels like *Jump Ship to Freedom*. In one scene, Daniel, a fugitive slave, speaks to a young black girl making her way down the street pushing a barrel filled with oysters:

As she went by, I grabbed her arm. "Say," I said.
    She stopped pushing the barrow and looked at me. "What?" she said.
    "I'm looking for the Congress. My master sent me down there

with a letter. He told me how to get there, but I forgot. I'm bound for a licking if I don't get there soon."

"I don't see no letter," she said.

"It's in my shirt," I said.

"Who's it for?"

"That ain't none of your business," I said.

"How'd you get your clothes all wet?" she asked.

"You're pretty nosy, ain't you?" She was younger than me. I wasn't going to take anything from her. (Collier and Collier 1981, 97)

As we discussed the excerpt we realized there was no jabber or the *hi*'s, *byes*, and *OKs* that often clutter dialogue in student writing. The talking has a purpose, showing Daniel's irritation with the little girl's spunky "nosiness." We discussed how Daniel feels when he finally says, "You're pretty nosy, ain't you?" We also noticed that the author describes movements as the characters talk, providing the reader with a fuller sense of the scene. We noted that Collier uses simple, unmodified "saids" to designate each speaker. Daniel doesn't need to "growl angrily," "That ain't none of your business" because the dialogue itself carries the emotion.

Students work on a story in progress with a partner next, underlining dialogue with a colored pencil. Writers take turns helping each other look for jabber, crossing out unnecessary *hi*'s and *byes*. They also make a note on the draft if they feel the story contains too much talking. We come back to this later in lessons and in conferences when we work together to rewrite characters, creating strategies to integrate description into nonstop dialogue.

RETHINKING WHAT YOU READ

When we read books together, discuss stories in small groups, or read independently, we continue to explore how authors use observations about people to create characters. This helps students read as writers, providing them with ongoing exposure to the craft of presenting characters through appearance, movement, and dialogue.

Often we simply discuss character presentation in our read-alouds; at other times we draw before we talk. In the middle of *Jump Ship to Freedom* (Collier and Collier 1981), we explored appearance, drawing the main character, Daniel; his mother; Big Tom; and Captain Ivers, Daniel's owner. But before we started, I reread excerpts describing how Big Tom has "muscles in his arms like straps of leather" (20) and Daniel works so hard "there was nothing to his palms but raw skin" (36).

As students drew I rotated from table to table, talking about how characters look. In these conversations writers learned why readers picture some characters better than others. Mustafa realized he had difficulty seeing the Captain because Collier "didn't say what he looked like" and Mustafa had "never seen a captain." He thought Captain Ivers "might look like a sailor with a hat, but I'm not sure." He pictured Daniel better because he remembered "his white shirt" and that "his pants got ripped" when Captain Ivers whipped him on board the *Junius Brutus*.

As students worked they also discovered that readers often fill in details authors omit: Sandy imagined that the Captain looked like "lots of guys like in old-fashioned days on TV . . . with short little jackets and stuff, all proper." Sophia remembered Big Tom's muscles and the scar across his face but added a belt and boots to her drawing "because that's the way I've seen sailors, kind of dressing like pirates."

I'm always looking for stories with unusual characters we can study and draw. One of my favorites is Madeleine L'Engle's (1962) classic fantasy, *A Wrinkle in Time*. I use a scene from the story describing a town full of characters who look and act alike:

> Below them the town was laid out in harsh angular patterns. The houses in the outskirts were all exactly alike, small square boxes painted gray. Each had a small, rectangular plot of lawn in front, with a straight line of dull-looking flowers edging the path to the door. . . . In front of all the houses children were playing. Some were skipping rope, some were bouncing balls. . . . As the skipping rope hit the pavement, so did the ball. As the rope curved over the head of the jumping child, the child with the ball caught the ball. Down came the ropes. Down came the balls. Over and over again. Up. Down. All in rhythm. All identical. Like the houses. Like the paths. Like the flowers. Then the doors of all the houses opened simultaneously and out came women like a row of paper dolls. The print of their dresses was different, but they all gave the appearance of being the same. . . . Each child turned and walked into the house. The doors clicked shut behind them. (103)

We read this excerpt several times, noting how balls, ropes, and movements are synchronized and uniform. We discuss how the author describes children catching "over and over again," how these movements make perfect sense in this strange fictional world. There's no dialogue in the scene, so I ask students to pretend they are on the sidewalk, watching and listening. First they draw what they picture; then they write what they see and hear. Jennifer thought the town was "like some weird movie." She wrote a scene

FIG. 3–6: Sandy's Character Illustrations for Jump Ship to Freedom

that followed a group of children into a house, using dialogue and action that mirrored the original characters' robotic behavior:

> Two boys were playing with the balls. They were passing it to each other. Then the girls were singing "Strawberry shortcake, cherry on top." All at the same time. Then all of the moms came outside. "Time to come in. It's dinner," all the moms said at the same time.

FIG. 3–7: Jennifer's Character Illustrations from A Wrinkle in Time

Then all the kids put their jump ropes and balls in the house. They all went up the stairs, step by step. All at the same time. They all went inside, sat on a chair at the same time. All the kids said, "What are we having for dinner?" The mom said, "Your favorite, liver!" Then all the kids jumped for joy. After dinner all the kids came back outside to play. They started turning the jump rope at the same time. All the boys were bouncing the balls at the same time.

Carlo's version was more like personal narrative. In the end, his actors broke character and commented on their "weird town":

I was in a strange town where kids were all playing the same thing. I could hear the jump rope smacking the ground and the ball hitting the ground. I could hear them all laughing and giggling. The houses were all gray and all the houses have only one flower. They were shining so bright. I hear one kid saying, "This town is weird. We all have the same houses." The other kid says, "Yeah, I know."

We continue to study character presentation when we read independently or in small groups. Sometimes before a conference, I ask students to write examples of actions, dialogue, or appearance on a Weekly Reading Focus. At other times I prepare formats to help them reflect before discussing ideas with a small circle of students reading the same book. This helps them apply what they learn to novels they read on their own, exploring how writers present characters in scenes and stories. It also supports our observations of dress, gesture, and talk, moving ten-year-olds toward a deeper understanding of the link between personal experience and fiction.

4

Rewriting Characters

> **Good Writers Know**
> Writers show appearance.
> Writers create meaningful dialogue.
> Writers show movement.
> Writers use movement and dialogue to reveal feelings.

Midway through the year our workshop begins to hum. Excited writers share drafts, brainstorm ideas, and start to practice the complex craft of creating unique and believable characters. In this process they explore how to present imaginary people through appearance, movement, speech, and thought, finding words to articulate what they previously implied, uncovering nuance and individuality.

I use demonstration lessons to help this process along, modeling ways I present characters in my own stories. I also confer with writers, helping them transfer what they learn in lessons to the characters they are developing in their ongoing work. We analyze stories and try out techniques, pondering when we need dialogue and when we don't, deciding if and where to add appearance and movement, and wondering what this tells the reader about the feelings and intentions of the people in our stories.

REWRITING APPEARANCE

When students first rewrite appearance, they often "front-load" information, listing clothing, age, and hair color at the very beginning of the piece. The revised lead to Mindy's "Odd World" is a typical example. She lists names, roles, and uniform colors for each character on "Lexx 3," a spaceship "sent out to find a new undiscovered planet and claim it for earth":

> Ten, nine . . . the countdown had started for Mindy and her crew aboard the Lexx 3. Mindy is the high commander. She is in charge of pretty much everything. Jennifer is "Panel Control." Emily is in charge of Sick Bay. Emily's uniform is baby blue. Mindy's uniform is Navy blue, and Jennifer's uniform is blue-green (aqua).

I try to show Mindy and other writers how to sprinkle appearance details into the story without disrupting the narrative flow. The year I wrote "The Race," I described how Emily, one of the main characters, stood on the school yard, "pushing her long, stringy hair tight behind her ear." In a demonstration lesson we discussed how this detail presents information without slowing down the action.

I often encourage writers to spend a day on their own, observing how particular people look and dress. Halfway through "Wash Up," Susan wasn't sure how to "get Mary to look like a real boy." I suggested she observe boys at school and make a list of boylike attributes. She and Marissa spent two recesses watching and writing, presenting their list of "Nike backpack" and "boxer shorts" in a share with Lori and Cindy the next day.

REWRITING DIALOGUE

Young writers overuse dialogue, often constructing stories as long, endless conversations. I model ways to add description to these pieces, converting some of the chatter to narration or action. In the following lesson I thought out loud about how I planned to revise a section of my race story because it contained too much talking:

Remember the part in my story when Emily and Maria are on the playground before the first race? Emily's really upset with Maria, feeling sort of jealous because Maria runs so fast? The two characters talk their way through the whole race. I was thinking about that last night. I don't think kids talk when they run, especially if they're really serious about winning. Also, because there's too much talking, I don't think I show the reader where the scene takes place. So I want to take out some of the dialogue and add description. Let me read that part again:

On the overhead projector:

"Hey, Maria, you think you're so fast. I bet I can beat you to the fence."
  "Try it!"
  "OK, let's go."
  "Hey, you're running faster than me."
  "Ha, ha. . . ."
  "Oops, my shoe's untied. Hey, no fair!"
  "Hey, you won. You cheated!"
  "I'm just faster than you!"
  "I want a rematch at lunch. And this time we need a referee."

I think I need to keep "Hey, Maria, you think you're so fast. I bet I can beat you to the fence" and "Try it" because this sets up the scene and shows that the characters are rivals, angrily challenging each other. But "OK, let's go" sounds like jabber to me. I mean, it just says what they *do*, they start to race. I think this dialogue slows down the story, and I can show this part better through action, with something like [I crossed out "OK, let's go" and added] "Emily lurched forward, lowering her head as she ran quickly past a group of girls exchanging candy near the steps. Maria followed, her lips tight, her eyes focused on the fence forty feet away." I like this because when Emily "lowers" her head and Maria keeps "her eyes focused on the fence" I show how the characters are determined to win. By saying that the fence is "forty feet away" I paint a better picture of the playground.

I also think I need to take out this whole part when they're running and talking. [I crossed out from "Hey, you're running faster than me" to "Oops, my shoe's untied. Hey, no fair!"] That doesn't make sense. I can describe the action here, saying, "Emily took long strides, pulling ahead of Maria as they neared the basketball court. Just as they reached the foul line, Emily glanced over her shoulder and saw Maria several yards behind, stooping to tie a shoe lace. Maria looked up frustrated, watching Emily grin as her hands slammed into the fence." I think my revision shows the race while adding information about "the basketball court" and "the foul line."

I like the last three lines of dialogue because I think they show that the problem's still not solved. Maria thinks Emily "cheated" and asks for a rematch. I think I'll strengthen the last line by adding movement to show Maria's feelings. I can add, "Emily kicked the asphalt with the tip of her sneakers. She glared at Emily" just before Maria says, "I want a rematch at lunch. And this time we need a referee."

I began the lesson discussing how Emily and Maria feel about each other, underscoring the idea that dialogue functions to reveal characters. As I proceeded, I explained that I kept the first two and last three lines because they show intention and motivation. I also discussed substituting description for dialogue during the race because it made sense and allowed me to show setting. Finally, I used Maria's angry "I want a rematch at lunch. And this time we need a referee" to model how to supplement dialogue with movement.

I referred to this lesson when Peter needed help with a similar dialogue dilemma. He came to me in November for a conference about his football piece. He'd written many stories during the first few months of school, producing new pieces every week or so. His hyperactivity and learning disability, however, made it difficult for him to focus on rewriting. He often set pieces aside or lost them as he rushed on to the next story, but when he liked something—and his behavior was under control—he harnessed his unbounded energy and love of writing to rethink, rework, and revise. I knew he was invested in "Peter's Football Fantasy" when he requested a conference, telling me he wanted to know "if it makes sense." As we talked we discovered that his piece contained too much confusing dialogue (dialogue underlined):

Peter read his story:

"Go, go! Please catch the ball. Please, this is for the game," I said. "He caught the ball but he's not at the touchdown yet," said Fred. "He has to shake people but you got to remember he's a running back. We only use him for this play, so I don't think he would get tackled that easy," I said.

   "Yep, you're right. But still, let's cheer for him."
   "Go, go!"
   "The 40, the 30, the 20! Oh no, he got tackled by Eddie Holloway."
   "OK, is Peter all right?"
   "I don't know."
   "Where am I?"
   "We only have ten yards for a first down left.
   "They're lining up in a shotgun position. I think they're using their special play."
   "Set, hike!"

Peter crossed Fred; Steven crossed Peter and Fred crossed Steven, so now the defense bumped into each other. Andrew passed the ball to Fred and he made the touchdown. "We're down by one. We need to make a two-point conversion."

> "Run this Peter. Please don't get tackled."
> "OK."
> Hike. Peter hands it off. He's running. He makes it.
> "We won!"

MS. J: "Go, go! Please catch the ball!" pulls me into your story right away. And I like how you focus on just a few plays at the end of the game. This creates drama. I'm wondering what you think you need to do next?

PETER: I don't think I show the action, like "swish, swish, he fell down."

MS. J: Where would you put that?

PETER [He silently read first page]: Right here, yeah, right around here after he gets tackled by Eddie Holloway.

He marked the part with six red stars.

MS. J: How would that help your story?

PETER: I think it would show more what he's doing.

MS. J: Why is it important to show what he's doing here?

PETER: It's telling about a main part of the story.

MS. J: That makes sense. Let's go through your story and underline the dialogue, so we can see how much talking you have already.

Peter underlined dialogue in green pencil. We spread the pages on the floor and continued our discussion.

MS. J: What do you think?

PETER: Well, there's action here [points to Hike . . .]

[pause]

MS. J: What about this part where you say "Peter crossed Fred?"

PETER: I think that's action, too.

MS. J: And what about the dialogue?

PETER: There's a lot of it . . . the players. They all talk.

Our conversation confirmed what Peter already knew. He told me right away that he needed to "show the action," and in the underlined pages he saw lots of talking and very little description. As we continued we discussed how I handled the same problem in my race story. Peter suggested he add something "about John getting in a fight with Eddie Holloway" and then went back to his table to rework this section of his piece.

The next day Peter announced that he "put in a fight," crossed out "OK, is Peter all right?" "I don't know. Where am I?" and made other changes. At this point I wanted him to add more action to his piece but knew he lacked the patience for another round of revision. In our final conference, we added dialogue designators to sort out who's talking and agreed that the final version of the story contained a better balance of talking and description [action underlined]:

"Go, go! Please catch the ball," Andrew said. "Please, this is for the game." <u>He caught the ball, but he did not get the touchdown yet.</u>

"He has to shake people but you got to remember, Andrew, he's a running back. We only use him for this play, so I don't think he would get tackled that easy."

"Yep, you're right, Mike, but still let's cheer for him."

<u>The forty, the thirty, the twenty. He got tackled by Eddie Holloway. He got up and pushed Eddie Holloway. The ref ran to break up the fight. Peter threw a punch, but one of the refs grabbed Peter's fist and he had to stay on the sidelines for ten minutes.</u>

"We only have ten yards for a first down," said Andrew.

"They're lining up in a shotgun position. I think they're using their special play involving Steven, Fred, and Peter," said the TV commentator up in the box.

<u>Peter crossed Fred. Steven crossed Peter and Fred crossed Steven, so now the defense bumped into each other. Andrew passed the ball to Fred and made the touchdown.</u>

"We are down by one. We need to make a two-point conversion," said the coach on the sidelines. "Run this, Peter. Please don't get tackled."

"He hands it off. He's running!" said the TV commentator again.

<u>Peter shook Eddie and he ran past Joseph for the conversion.</u> "We win the game to go to the Super Bowl!"

Ronnie's "Off Road Race" also contained line after line of dialogue, but, unlike Peter, Ronnie didn't recognize this at the beginning of our conference. I asked him to underline the talking so we could discuss what he had done and decide what to do next. His underlined first draft looked like this:

One evening Paulo and Ronnie had two off-road Huffer tanks. Paulo's was black and Ronnie's was white. They went to the duck pond where there was [*sic*] rocks and mud. They both charged it up to as fast as it [*sic*] can go.

<u>"Start the countdown. 5, 4, 3, 2, 1, GO!"</u>

<u>"He he! Yours fell in the water," said Ronnie.</u>

<u>"No!" replied Paulo.</u>

<u>"Yes, yes, yes! You lost!</u>

<u>"No, it's coming back again."</u>

<u>"Who you calling a loser? Yours ran into a tree!"</u>

<u>"What!"</u>

<u>"Look at yours. Now it's stuck in a tree."</u>

"I'll be back with my chain saw."
"What?"
"Never mind."
"There, I'm back."
"Where'd you go?"
"For the last time, I went to get my chain saw."
"ZZZZZZZZZZ"
"I'm coming."
"What?"
"SNAP"
"We forgot to make the finish line. Ah, ha, here's a stick."
"OK, Go!"
"No!"
"Yes!"
"No!"
"Yes!"
"No!"
"Yes!" said Paulo and Ronnie
It was a tie.
"I want a rematch!"said Paulo.

Like Peter, Ronnie discovered by underlining that the characters "mostly talk" after he set the scene in the lead to his story. Later in the conference we discussed removing unnecessary talk, and over the next few days, Ronnie deleted much of the jabber, including the tree and chain-saw incident which he decided "isn't part of the point of the story."

One evening Paulo and Ronnie had two off-road Huffer tanks. Paulo's was black and Ronnie's was white. They went to the duck pond where there was [sic] mud and rocks. They both charged the tanks up to as fast as it [sic] can go.
"Start the countdown. 5, 4, 3, 2, 1, GO!"
"SLASH"
"Oh, oh, looks like you're a loser!"
"No, I'm not!" replied Paulo.
"Then pick it up out of the water and put it on the ground."
"OK, Okey-dokey [sic], she's . . .hey, it worked. I'm racing up to you."
"What?
Stop! We forgot to make the finish line!"
"Dah, here's a stick."
"OK, Go!"

> "No!"
> "Yes!"
> "No!"
> "Yes!"
> "No!"
> "Yes," said Ronnie and Paulo.
> It was a tie.
> "I want a rematch!" said Paulo.

Ronnie focused the second draft on the drama of the race, cutting out a half page of distracting conversation. In our next conference we talked about changing some remaining dialogue into description to help readers see the setting. I jotted down on a Post-it, "Page 3: Take out some talking and show actions instead." Ronnie went off to rewrite but seemed a little confused. A few days later he asked for another conference:

MS. J: How's it going?

RONNIE: I've been thinking about how to make the last part all action, but when I started to do it, it was hard.

MS. J: Do you understand what you were supposed to do?

RONNIE: Try to make it longer . . . to extend it . . . like right here.

MS. J: Why do we need to do that?

RONNIE: 'Cause it was too much dialogue, right here and here.

MS. J: I'll help you get started. Let's go through and see what dialogue we want to keep. We'll look for talking that shows how the characters feel. How about "Start the countdown: 5, 4, 3, 2, 1, Go!" Does that show how they feel about each other?

RONNIE: No, I don't think so. It's just how they count it down.

MS. J: How could we change that to a description of action?

[long pause]

MS. J: Who's talking here?

RONNIE: It's Paulo.

MS. J: Then how could you just say that he counts down?

RONNIE: Somebody, Pauol counts down . . . or Paulo starts the countdown.

MS. J: Sure, something like that. What's happening when you say "Go?"

RONNIE: That's when they start the race.

MS. J: How can you show us that without saying "Go"?

RONNIE: They put the tanks on the ground and they took off.

MS. J: Why don't you write that right now.

Ronnie crossed out "Go" and wrote "They put the tanks on the ground."

MS. J: And "Splash," what happens there?

RONNIE: Ronnie's keeps on going and Paulo's went off in the water.

MS. J: Well, you can write that. Let's look at the next line. "Oh, no, looks like you're a loser!" Does this show Ronnie's feelings toward Paulo?

RONNIE: I think that shows that Ronnie thinks he's a loser.

MS. J: I agree. It shows Ronnie's feelings, so maybe it would be good to leave that part in.

As we began our conference I learned that Ronnie knew that he had written too much dialogue but wasn't sure how to change it. It's tricky business, so I took him through his piece, line by line, double underlining essential talking, dialogue that shows feelings. At the same time I helped Ronnie verbalize the actions underlying less essential talking so he understood how to convert "Go" to "They put the tanks on the ground" and the "'Yes, No'" sequence to "The tanks kept going back and forth."

This seemed to help. Ronnie worked on these changes for about a week, completing the final draft just before spring break:

> Ronnie and Paulo went to the duck pond where there was [sic] rocks and mud. They both charged the off-road Huffer tanks up to as fast as it [sic] can go. Paulo started the countdown. They put the tanks on the ground. They watched Ronnie's going on the mud and Paulo's splashing in the water. <u>"Oh, no, looks like you are a loser."</u> <u>"No, I'm not!" replied Paulo. "Okey-dokey [sic], sheeez!"</u> Paulo stooped down to pick it up. He put his hand in the water and felt around until he felt it. Paulo had it in his hand, so he put it on the ground and he let it go again. <u>"Hey, it worked. I'm catching up to you."</u> Paulo looked over to see the finish line. It wasn't there so he went to find a stick. Ronnie kept watching the race. Paulo ran back to Ronnie, and said he had a stick for the finish line. The tanks keep [sic] going, back and forth. Ronnie's tank caught up to Paulo's, and it stayed with Paulo's tank, and they stayed together until the finish line. <u>Paulo said, "I want a rematch!"</u>

REWRITING MOVEMENT

When I help writers add gestures and body movements to expand and dramatize a scene, I talk them through the action, clarifying what the characters do in each part of the scenario. I did this with Peter after we decided on a focus for his rambling, five-chapter "school story," which he wrote during the first two weeks of writers' workshop. He put it aside for a month, sharing it with Steven one day when he "couldn't think of anything else to write." Steven told him that "it's great" but he needed to "focus it better." Patrick said he liked the "camping part best" but didn't offer advice on how to make this a complete story. Peter put the piece aside again, ignoring it for several weeks while he churned out several stories about basketball, Yosemite, and two lost boys. Finally, he brought it to a conference, and we identified five potential stories: "all my friends," "playground fight," "school camping trip," "bus ride," and "going fishing." We talked about Steven's comments, and, by the end of our discussion, Peter decided that the "fishing part" would make the best story:

Peter read the "fishing" chapter:

Me and Patrick started to go fishing and all we caught was perch for an hour or two. But me and Patrick saw a giant catfish and we were in luck because we had liver and we stuck it on the hook and he snapped at it twice in a row and me and Patrick tried to pull him in but we couldn't pull him in. "Oh, no! He pulled Patrick in. Oh, no, what's going to happen to me? What will happen to me if I return without him. I have to save him." So I dived down to save him and I couldn't find him. "Oh, no, I can't find him. What am I going to do? Oh, I need some air." I took a breath and I went back under. "Oh, there he is. I've got to save him. Ugggh! Ugggh! He's too heavy. Mike, Mike, wake up. He's gained consciousness. Swim, swim. Good." After we got up we went back to camp.

MS. J: Why do you like this part best?

PETER: It has action.

MS. J: Like . . .

PETER: When Patrick drowns and I try to save him. Oh yeah . . . catching the fish.

MS. J: I like it when you say "I took a breath and I went back under." You show what you are doing; you take a breath and dive under again. Are there other places where you can show how the characters move?

PETER: I'm not. . . . Well, maybe when he goes in the water.

MS. J: When he first tried to save him?

PETER: Yeah.

MS. J: Let's find that part.

Peter reread his piece to himself.

PETER: Maybe around here someplace [pointed to top of page 2, from "What will happen" to "I need some air"].

MS. J: That seems like a good place, especially when you say, "So I dived down to save him and I couldn't find him." I think you can expand this, showing us how the character moves into the water and what he does to try to find Patrick.

In the first draft of his story Peter entered the mind of his character, showing us how he struggled for breath as he searched for his friend. I pointed out how he detailed going "under" the water in the drowning scene, encouraging him to find other places where he might add movements to help us picture this drama. He found a place at the top of the second page, and I identified a specific sentence to rethink and expand. As our conversation continued he said he wasn't sure what to write, so we reread the drowning scene from *On My Honor*, noting how the author showed Joel "pulling himself forward and under with both arms, his eyes open and smarting in the murky water" (Bauer 1986, 32). We talked through the possibilities in his story:

MS. J: What happens as you dive into the water?
PETER: There might be some fish.
MS. J: Put yourself in the water. What do you see or feel?
PETER: The fish are around my legs.
MS. J: Anything else?
PETER: Some moss gets around my face.

We verbally constructed the rest of the scene. I wrote some of our ideas on a Post-it, and Peter returned to his table to revise his story. The next day, he deleted "I couldn't find him. 'Oh, no, I can't find him. What am I going to do? Oh, I need some air,'" replacing it with:

I felt fish around my legs and moss around my head and it felt like the fish were carrying me through the water. "It's hopeless. He's probably all the way across the lake by now."

We talked about the rest of the piece, especially the part where Peter saves Patrick. When Peter left this conference, he told me he wanted to "write everything over" after "I took a breath, and I went back under." He took *On My Honor* back to his table, reading it again the next day during quiet write. Over the next few workshops he rewrote the end of the story, modeling some of it after Bauer's scene:

I saw a shape that looked like Patrick. I was not sure because I could not see very well and there was moss around my face and eyes. I felt my eyes starting to hurt and sting, so I closed my eyes but I felt my heart beating harder and faster and my lungs needed air so I went back up and I gasped for as much air as I could. I went back under and I saw him!! I swam over there in a rush. I grabbed his arm and tried to pull him up to the deck. But he was not moving. I tried to figure out what was wrong. There was a vine stuck to his foot so I went back up to get the knife from the tackle box. I went back under and cut it off and we swam back. "Peter," Patrick screamed, "thanks, Peter, I almost died. They went back to the camp in relief.

Peter used movement and dialogue to show desperation and eventual relief as his main character plays out the drama of saving a drowning friend. In his revised story we feel his character's "heart beating harder and faster" as he "gasps" for air, "grabbing" Patrick's arm and attempting to pull him out of the water. Action and dialogue finally reveal his character's intentions after weeks of discussions and rewrites.

REWRITING MOTIVATION

I work all year helping writers see the connection Peter makes between doing, talking, and feeling. Again, I use my stories to show students how to do this. In the following lesson, I analyzed a short section of "The Race" to see what it revealed about my characters' emotions:

Today I'm going to read over my story and see how I show my character's feelings. I want Emily to dislike Maria at the beginning. By the end, they're friends. I'll look at how they talk to each other when they first meet. It's here on the second page, just after Emily sees Maria run for the first time:
On the overhead projector:

Maria entered the classroom by herself, hesitating for a moment before she took a seat kitty-corner to Emily's table. She opened her notebook and whispered, "Do you have an extra pencil?"
Emily flushed and stared down at her book. Maria asked again, and this time Emily stood up and walked to the classroom library. Maria watched her as she crossed the room.

I write "Emily flushed and stared down at her book." She doesn't answer Maria. She walks away. I think this shows that she's angry, maybe jealous and doesn't like Maria. But I also want Maria to show that she's irritated by this. I don't think "Maria watched her as she crossed the room" shows this. I could add talking, a facial expression, maybe a gesture, or some other movement here. I think I'll have Maria tap her desk with her finger. I'll add it, here, after "crossed the room."

On the overhead I added "Maria tapped her finger on desk and looked up at Ms. Jordan, who'd just begun to take attendance."

I began the lesson talking about my characters, again emphasizing that human emotion drives good stories. I analyzed each line and decided what it showed about feelings. I concluded by modeling how to add gesture to enhance my character's sense of rejection and indignation.

In conferences I use similar strategies to help writers understand how emotions underlie action. We examine short segments of text, discussing character perception and intention. Sandy, for instance, knew that intense feelings between Jenny and Michelle drive the plot in "Lip Gloss, " telling me that " Michelle not liking Jenny" is the story problem. She was less sure whether she showed this in her writing. We talked about how her characters felt in our very first conference:

SANDY: I think I tell how she feels in this part when . . . See, she hates Michelle. She says her story isn't good [pointed to "How can Jenny's story ever be good?"].

MS. J: Do you show her feelings in any other place?

SANDY: Maybe here where she says "Who cares, just read!"

MS. J: So you show us through . . .

SANDY: Dialogue.

MS. J: How about Jenny? How do we find out how she feels?

SANDY: When she goes to the share to read her story?

MS. J: How is she feeling then?

SANDY: Kind of nervous.

MS. J: Let's read that part and see.

She read: "Jenny pulled out her chair, swinging her arms taking long strides so she could get to [the] rug before anyone."

MS. J: How do you feel when you take long strides to get to the rug?

SANDY: Excited, maybe, wants to get there first. I don't think it makes sense because she's scared. . . . I probably could change it.

MS. J: How?

SANDY: Maybe she could take little steps.

MS. J: She could. How else could she show that she's scared?

SANDY: She could get red in the face . . . maybe, or bite her nails.

As we worked through her piece Sandy recognized that "striding" suggests confidence and excitement. In her final draft she changed this to "takes baby steps" and further dramatized Jenny and Michelle's conflict by adding details to show Jenny "blushing like a red balloon" and Michelle explaining to another character that Jenny "is always in my face."

Media-based characters present similar challenges. Jacob modeled "Where Is It? Where Is It?" after the cartoon *Garfield*. When he watches it on TV, he notices "what happens," not how Garfield feels. In this conference we started at the beginning of the story, examining "what happens" and clarifying Garfield's intentions as we read:

Jacob read his story:

Garfield was looking for a pan for Jon to make his lasagna. Garfield looked everywhere. He looked in the closet and he could see a black outline of a box. Garfield stepped on the outline and fell through a trap door. He landed in a room with lots of gadgets on the wall and a car with skis for tires. There were other gadgets on the car. Garfield pressed a red button on the car and the skis on the car slid up in the car. The car fell with a thud. Garfield pressed the red button again. The skis came out and lifted the car. Garfield pressed on a green button on the car and Garfield started seeing things on the screen like going on a diet and going to the vet. Garfield quickly pressed the button again and he stopped seeing things. Garfield said, "These buttons on the car are nothing but trouble."

Garfield walked over to the wall and pressed a button that said on it "Door." The door to the car opened and Garfield walked in. The door closed behind him. Garfield looked at the dashboard of the car. He saw lots of buttons, so Garfield pressed one. The car started to move fast and the second he let go of the button, the door slid open. Garfield walked out of the car and he looked around. He was in another room. Then he saw a pan! But the pan was guarded by a robot. Garfield had a mirror in his pocket. He started shining it so it reflected the sun. It shined in the robot's eyes. The robot put his hands over his eyes and screamed. While the robot screamed, Garfield ran through the robot's legs and got the pan and ran to the door.

The robot saw Garfield run to the door. The robot took out a laser gun and said," Die, die, die!" He shot the laser but it bounced off the mirror and hit the robot. Garfield ran back to the car again and spotted an intercom with a button. Garfield pressed the button and said, "Jon, is that you? If it is, turn on the oven because I'm coming home!"

MS. J: Let's start with this part, when Garfield sees the trap door? What's happening?

JACOB: He sees this outline and it's, you know, you can see the trap door.

MS. J: What's he feeling when he sees it?

JACOB: I think he's (Garfield), uh, maybe scared. I guess scared when he falls through the floor. He felt. . . . I . . . hum . . . I should put "He said to himself, 'I don't think I should do this.'"

MS. J: And then after he falls through the trapdoor, he feels. . . .

JACOB: I guess he feels anxious about the pan because he likes lasagna.

MS. J: How could you show us he is anxious?

MS. J: You could tell us that, but could you show us through an action? Think about it. What would he do if he were anxious?

JACOB: He could, like, run around the car looking and running.

Jacob matched actions with feelings in this conference, discovering the emotions that motivate Garfield to open a hidden trap door in search of a lasagna pan. We briefly discussed the difference between telling action and showing it by making Garfield "run around the car." Later, when Jacob was stuck on his ending, he thought through the action again, constructing a scene using movements and dialogue to show Jon's irritation and Garfield's relief to be back in the kitchen just in time for lunch.

For lengthy stories I ask writers to take a separate sheet of paper, read through the piece, and list feelings, action by action. Lori did this for Susan, the main character in "The Land Under the Bathtub." We worked from the draft of her twelve-page story, which began like this:

> I was in the bathroom starting to brush my teeth when I heard a sound. "Clink, clink, clink." I stepped over to the bathtub. I saw the same shiny white bathtub that my family had for years. When I turned around I got a glimpse of something in the bathtub. I stepped into the bathtub and looked closer at the black spot that's no bigger than a mouse hole. The black spot looked a lot like a hole to me so I stuck my finger inside. Suddenly, the whole room turned black. I felt myself falling. I reached for something to cling to but nothing was in reach. Little sparks of light flashed in front of my eyes. I felt my skin getting tighter and tighter. The wind was roaring in my ears like a hurricane. Finally, I landed with a thud. When I got up, I felt like I'd been falling for an hour. I looked at my watch which I always took off just before going to sleep. It was 12:30. I would have been reading my chapter book right now.
>
> I looked around the place that I landed on. I was no longer in my family's bathtub. There was a stem about a few feet away. The place smelled like chocolate. There were lots of flowers around me, but I didn't see any people. . . .

We read through the first page together, starting a list that Lori would finish by herself. She spent two days reviewing the rest of the piece. She listed over twenty emotions, including how Susan feels "sleepy" when she's "in the bathroom starting to brush (her) teeth" and "curious" when she hears a "clink, clink, clink" sound coming from the bathtub. In a follow-up conference, we discussed the ups and downs of Susan's journey and how her sleepiness turned to worry by the end of the story.

Lori created a typical list: most kid-generated characters exhibit simple, unidimensional emotions. On occasion, however, writers create complex characters, characters who present contradictory or ambivalent feelings. In Jessica and Olivia's collaboration, " Why Did You Leave," a young girl's guilt and sense of loss over her father's suicide drives the story. Jessica and Olivia came to understand the complexity of their characters' emotions in a series of peer shares and conferences.

This was Jessica's first collaboration with Olivia, a less prolific but passionate writer who had produced a series of personal narratives starring herself and her older brother, Daniel. They brought an unfinished draft of "Why Did You Leave" to me in October, wanting to know if it made sense:

Jessica and Olivia took turns reading. See story, Chapter 1.

MS. J: What do you think about it?

OLIVIA: I think it's good.

JESSICA: I'm not sure if it makes sense. About the dad and the mom. I mean, the dad kills himself.

MS. J: Why does he kill himself?

JESSICA: Because he thinks he's bad.

MS. J: Why?

JESSICA: Because he was mean to his daughter.

MS. J: How was he mean?

OLIVIA: He hit her.

MS. J: How about the mom? Why does she want to kill the daughter?

JESSICA: 'Cause she looks like the dad.

I wondered as they read if they would abandon this piece. I knew it would take a long time to write and require multiple peer and teacher conferences. The story premise presented a huge challenge, dealing with child abuse and complex, unpleasant human emotion. I felt somewhat uncomfortable with this but thought the girls were up to the challenge, so I decided to begin by exploring motivation, helping Jessica and Olivia define how these complex characters feel about each other. I also wanted them to show, not tell, this story, so later in the conference we talked about seeing out of Sherry's eyes, showing us the park and immediately drawing us into

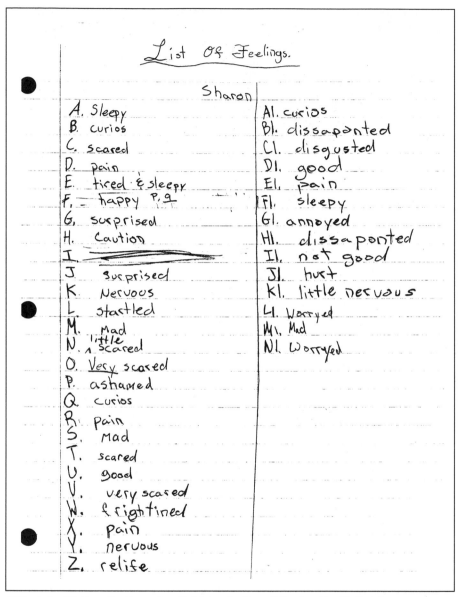

FIG. 4–1: *Listing Feelings: Lori's Notes for* Land Under the Bathtub

Sherry's complex dilemma. Olivia and Jessica agreed that [the] "girl was sitting in the park with her mom" wasn't as interesting as Olive's suggested new lead, "Gloomy, gloomy . . . she sat on a bench, a green bench next to her mother." I wrote, "How does Sherry feel about her dad? How does the dad feel about her?" on a Post-it and the girls spent the rest of the week working on revisions. At one point, Olive introduced the idea of "day dreaming" as a device to present more information about the dad:

JESSICA: I was thinking she could see her dad everywhere.

OLIVIA: In her imagination . . . when she was dreaming about him, what he did to her and stuff.

JESSICA: . . . or when she looks inside a mirror.

OLIVIA: She goes into her dream and looks at her dad and then she jumps up off the bench.

JESSICA: She's day-dreaming. . . .

OLIVIA: Yeah, and she jumps up and her mom says, "What's happening?" and she says, "Nothing, nothing."

After they rewrote the lead, they signed up for a whole group share to "see if the kids like it." The story created a flurry of responses, mostly about the dad:

AZAR: You need to say he kills himself because he's a bad dad.

JESSICA: We didn't do that yet.

BETH: I don't get the part about throwing stuff out the window.

OLIVIA: That's when they want to forget about the dad.

JESSICA: They throw his stuff out.

STEVEN: I don't get why he thought he was a bad dad because hitting a child is bad but grabbing them and disciplining them is OK. I don't know why he would kill himself because he hit his own child.

JESSICA: He didn't . . .

OLIVIA: He killed himself because he didn't really mean to hit her. . . . he was drunk and he hit the girl. He walked up to her like a man living on the street. He didn't know what he was doing.

PATRICK: Take the dad out of the story.

JESSICA: He couldn't control himself.

JACOB: When does this take place? It sounds like a history story where people beat their children, but you say they go to an apartment. Wouldn't she just go to the police?

Writers reacted strongly to this story. Some seemed angry, others distressed as if we were talking about real children, real abuse, real feelings.

Patrick was so disturbed by the dad that he suggested the girls "take him out." Jessica and Olivia left the discussion somewhat bewildered, perhaps realizing for the first time that they had embarked on a difficult and complicated project. Jacob, Steven, and Beth raised important issues: Why does the father hate Sherry? Do modern dads act this way? Why don't they just call the police? In a small-group share several days later, Lori, Sandy, and Michelle continued to question whether the characters in this story made sense:

LORI: Why did he hit her?
JESSICA: Because he hated her, not really hated her but he didn't really like her.
LORI: Why didn't he like her? She's his daughter.
JESSICA: I don't know.
LORI: Maybe he hit her 'cause she looked like him.
SANDY: And he hated himself! Does he like the mommy?
OLIVIA: Yeah.
SANDY: What happened to the part where the mom wants to kill the daughter?
JESSICA: That is from the other draft.
MICHELLE: What's going to happen? What's the story problem?
JESSICA: This little girl had a father, but the father's dead.
SANDY: A story problem is the thing that's wrong in the story and you have to . . .
MICHELLE: You have to solve the problem.
JESSICA: The story problem is that her parents didn't like her. . . .

The girls discussed Sherry's family for a few more minutes and then, at the end of the workshop, set the story aside. About a week later Jessica retrieved the piece and, working quietly by herself, began the next round of revisions. She added that "Sherry was daydreaming about her dad because he was mean to her and hit her all the time." At this point, Jessica and Olivia seemed to understand the dad, but I wondered what they thought about Sherry. I explored this in our next conference:

MS. J: I see you've reworked your lead.
JESSICA: Yeah, we put in stuff about the park.
MS. J: You added how the dad was mean to Sherry. I'm wondering how she feels about this?
JESSICA: She's sad and mad that he's dead.
MS. J: How does she feel about the dad hitting her?

JESSICA: At first she thought he was going to be a nice man, but he turned out to be a bad man. That makes her sad.

MS. J: Does she have other feelings?

OLIVIA: Angry because when he hits her, she feels like hitting him back, like crying and sad, too.

MS. J: Sounds like Sherry feels sad and mad at the same time.

Jessica and Olivia discovered Sherry's mixed feelings in this discussion. Sherry is ambivalent, "sad and mad at the same time." This makes sense but further complicates the girls' task, especially when they attempt to devise a solution to this complex story problem. The girls continued to revise, "fixing up the mom part" and changing the lead:

> It was a gloomy day at the park. Sherry was daydreaming on a green bench with her mom. Her brother and her sister were playing in the sandbox. She had to sit out because she threw sand in Nick's hair. Nick is her brother. Sherry was daydreaming about her dad. How he was mean to her and how he hit her all the time and he had killed himself with a gun a year ago. Sherry thought he was a mean man and he thought he was a bad man. When he hit her, she felt like hitting him back and she was sort of mad and sad from him hitting her. She felt like a payback.

Jessica and Olivia worked for another week, meeting again with Lori and Sandy to discuss the "payback" idea (see Chapter 1). Then Jessica told me that they might abandon the story because they couldn't think of an ending. Sherry's "sad" and "mad," and her dad's dead. This was tricky. How could they bring this complex story to a satisfactory close? I suggested they meet with other writers and brainstorm a solution. Finally, a few days later, Jessica showed me a list "about a dream Sherry can have," a dream in which she meets her dad and they forgive each other. "A really great idea," she told me, inspired by something she dreamt over the weekend. For the next three weeks, Jessica and Olivia wrote the dream scene, completing a final draft after two on-and-off months of difficult writing:

> It was a gloomy day at the park when Sherry was daydreaming on a green bench with her mom. Her brother and two sisters were playing in the sandbox. She had to sit out because she threw sand in her brother Nick's hair. Sherry was daydreaming about her dad. She could daydream about a lot of things, like how he would hit

her. He would hit her because he was drunk. It was hard to live with him because he was mean and smelled bad not taking a bath. Sherry's mother would always tell him to take a bath. He would say, "No, I'm watching TV." They would get in a fight. Lori, the mother, said she was going to call the police, so Daniel, the dad, ran off in his car. He was gone for a long time. He was dead, a cop told them.

Lori cried for days thinking of what she had done wrong. She thought she could not love her kids. They moved to Alameda. Once they got there they started to unpack their things. They found a box with all of their pictures with their dad. They burned the pictures of him.

It was about 10:45 at night, so Sherry had to go to bed. She went to bed and fell asleep. She had a dream. She saw herself in a red velvet dress. She looked down at her red velvet shoes. She knew that she couldn't afford them. She started to dance around and she leaped. She looked down and saw a note. She read the note: "You will go through a castle, then come to a town. All the people will look like your father." Then the grass opened and she went down the stairs. She saw one more note that said, "If you want to finish the dream, tell your dad how you feel about him leaving." A branch opened. She saw her dad running away from her. She followed him. She came to a castle. She got in the castle and found the guards asleep. She tiptoed over one guard's shoe. She jumped and landed on her feet. The guards heard the shoes when the shoes hit the ground. They got up. They could not catch up.

She got out of the castle. She came to a town. The people all looked like her daddy. She saw a sign that said, "Come in and see the Mayor of the town." Sherry crossed the street and turned. She came to a building. She went up the ladder to the fifth floor. She saw a man running away from her. She followed him. They were locked in a room together. She looked at him like she was going to cry. "Why did you leave, Dad?" He said, "Do you remember when your grandpa died in the fire?" "No, I don't," said Sherry. "Will you tell me the story?" "OK," said dad, so they sat down on the couch together. "Your grandpa was in the bathroom. The house was burning down. He did not know until the fire came in the bathroom. He jumped out of the window. He ran to the water and after he cooled down, he died. Since I was so close to my father, I didn't want to lose him so I killed myself." "I feel it was wrong that you died and that you were mean to me." "I'm sorry, but sorry can't do anything. But it's just how life has to be."

"Wake up, wake up!" said Sherry's sister Judy who was shaking her. Sherry woke up as happy as can be.

Jessica and Olivia struggled to rewrite characters in "Why Did You Leave." Through discussions with others they brought Sherry and her dad to center stage, showed their complex feelings, gave them life, and made them more believable. In this process, they addressed other important story elements. When they revised the lead, they helped us picture the setting, the park where the drama begins. They deleted "payback" and other ideas that cluttered the plot. They did what good writers do: in rewriting characters, they showed places, clarified events, and pulled us into the heart of the story.

5

Refining the Story

Good Writers Know

Writers use mental landscapes to create settings.
Writers gather information to picture unfamiliar settings.
Writers discover plot.
Writers construct logical plots.
Writers create a focus or conflict for the plot.
Stories have meaning.

VISUALIZING SETTING

MS. J: I see you've started a new story.

MICHELLE: Yeah, it's about these teenagers that go in a haunted house and get killed.

MS. J: Can you picture the house?

MICHELLE: It's the house on Central, up the street. I walk by it on the way to school.

MS. J: What does it look like?

MICHELLE: It has these big, long windows and it's dark inside. An old crazy lady lives there. There's trash, and the paint's all chipped up. These stairs, they've got a bunch of stuff on it [*sic*]. They look like you'd fall if you walk on them. Me and Lori think it's haunted.

Michelle went on to tell me that she decided to write a story about the house that morning as she, Lori, and Lori's little sister walked to school. She mentioned the house in the fifth sentence, saying, "They decided to go into the house. There were cobwebs hanging on the ceiling." Where's the description of the place that inspires the story? It remained in Michelle's imagination as she dramatized the action. Like most fifth-graders, she ignored the setting, moving her characters from the porch to a bedroom and back to the street, naming but not showing these places, though she clearly pictured them in her mind.

Michelle and other fifth-graders approach settings the way they approach characters: they know them but don't show them. I spent a number of years exploring this observation with Kira Walker, a colleague of mine at Washington School. We discovered that kids imagine more than they write and often don't "see" the setting at all. In most cases they create incidental backdrops for action-packed narratives, basing these settings on sounds, smells, images, textures, feelings, attitudes, and stories associated with places they visit, see in the media, or learn about from books or other people. Sometimes these backdrops replicate real places; sometimes they're synthesized from many sources.[1] Like the house in Michelle's story, writers name or imply settings, providing only a glimpse of the mental landscapes used to create them. Unlike adult writers who consciously use "a system of place symbolism" (Lutwach 1984, 41) to create physical contexts for fiction, ten-year-olds rarely ponder how size, location, centrality, light, and atmosphere support and extend a story.

Nevertheless, it always strikes me that young writers construct simple backdrops that make story sense. Intuitively, place and plot complement each other. Michelle's house on Central Street is "haunted"—a place associated with decay and death, the perfect place for teen characters to meet an early demise. Similarly, the miniature waterworld Lori creates under the bathroom floor in "The Land Under the Bathtub" is the perfect place to trap a young hero, a place filled with talking flowers and flash floods initiated by runoff from family showers in the world above.

There's also a logic to the way Lori, Michelle, and other young writers string places together in stories. Michelle moves characters from the street to the porch to interior rooms, constructing a simple pattern of place-to-place movement to support the action. As in Tony's "Camp Horror" or Patrick and Jacob's "Keep it Unlocked," characters move to increasingly dangerous places and are stranded or dead by the end of the story. In each piece they begin this journey in safety—on the street, at a bus stop, in a bedroom. Michelle's teenagers die in an upstairs bedroom; Tony saves his trio at the "haunted" camp but puts them back on the bus to relive the experience the next summer; Patrick and Jacob's pair end up dead on the living room floor after a scary chase down the stairs and into the hallway; and Lori's hero in "Land Under the Bathtub" leaves the comfort of her house to spend the rest of her life in a miniature waterworld hidden away in the floorboards of her bathroom. What better way to scare readers than to lead characters from the security of familiar rooms and streets to the danger of scary camps and hostile hidden places?

Ten-year-olds use other patterns, too. Many construct *bed-to-bed* settings, beginning and ending adventures in the relative safety of a house or some other *home base*. In Mustafas's "Garry and Matt" the story begins and ends in the mouse hole after a harrowing trip across the kitchen floor in search of the cheese. Ricky and Tommy's "Horror Me or Curse Me" opens in a young boy's bedroom. He hears his mother call, "Kat, wake up. You're going to be late for school." As the story proceeds Kat leaves the house and, instead of going to school, walks to the beach, where he encounters a giant sea creature that chases him through back roads and alleys until he finally reaches the safety of his fenced-in yard. Lutwach identifies similar narrative motifs in adult fiction when heroes journey "from a central place to a number of outlying places and from them back to the starting place." This creates "a feeling of stability and completion" (Lutwach 1984, 43), a happily-ever-after closure satisfying to grownups and children alike.

These patterns, the intuitive logic that governs young writers, informs the way I teach story setting. Through conferences and lessons, we learn to show setting the way we learn to rewrite characters, using what we know to visualize places and rethink stories. In a sense, we investigate our flat, two-dimensional backdrops, give them substance, shape, and color, learning to use them to support story drama.

Exploring Landscapes

I begin our study of setting with a group lesson, asking each writer to list the settings used in a current story. We collate this information on the chalkboard, usually discovering that most of the action takes place at school, or in homes, malls, and other familiar landscapes. I often follow up with a home assignment, asking students to watch a TV program and list the settings again. We collate results in class, contrasting and comparing our findings.

I then demonstrate how I construct places in my own pieces. Some time ago I wrote a mystery about two young tourists visiting Tahiti, basing the plot on a trip I'd taken the summer before. In my lesson I recalled images, sounds, and smells from my trip and modeled techniques for integrating these ideas into the story:

I think I need to describe the setting better in my Tahiti story, especially the part where the two girls get lost on their way back from dinner. Here's what I wrote:

I referred to text written on overhead transparency:

"Jackie and Rachel walked down the dark road. It only took a few minutes before the girls realized that they were lost." I don't think a reader pictures this scene very well. I say that they walked down a "dark road," but I don't give any detail about the road or the surrounding area. I also could say more about how dark it was, like what they could see. If I did this, I would strengthen the scary mood or feeling of this scene. I think that's important because the rest of the story is about finding their way to the hotel.

Thus, I need to think back to my trip and try to picture this road. I remember how shocked I felt when we walked out of a restaurant at 6:00, and it was pitch black. We couldn't see beyond the single lamp that lit up the sign on the front of the building. A half circle of light went out about ten or twelve feet in front of us and that was it. The clouds hid the moon, and there weren't any street lights. In fact, there was one main road, and every once in a while—about every ten minutes or so—someone would come buzzing down the road in a small French car lighting the street for just enough time to walk a few yards. When the cars sped by, we could see the asphalt and the white line down the center. We also got a glimpse of the grass-lined ditch on the side. It was really hard to see it, but I remember that the grass was tall, about up to our knees. It had the damp smell of water that had been there a long time and had garbage in it. The ditch looked deep, five or six feet down, and sometimes the headlights reflected off rivulets of water that trickled over rocks and mud on the side. All the time I was afraid one of us would slip down the muddy slope into the ditch, which one of the locals told us was filled with huge rats.

Now, I don't want to put all of this in my story, but I think I should describe what my characters can see in the dark and maybe put in something about the ditch. I'll start by looking out of their eyes as they leave the restaurant, thinking as I write about what I saw when I was there. I want to show how dark it is:

I crossed out "Jackie and Rachel walked down the dark road" and wrote:

Jackie and Rachel stopped abruptly as they opened the door to leave the restaurant. It was pitch black. They couldn't see anything beyond the circle formed by the porch light directly above their heads. As they ventured into the darkness a car sped by, quickly illuminating the asphalt and the broken white line down the center of the road. The car passed and the road darkened again. "Let's walk along the side near the ditch. If enough cars come by, we should be able to see our way back."

In this part, I describe the darkness that Jackie and Rachel see. I think I'll use an action, now, to show the ditch. I can make one of the characters slip but not fall in:

Rachel led the way. As they approached the edge of the road Jackie's shoe caught a rock. Her foot slipped down the muddy slope, through the grass that brushed against her knee as she grabbed Rachel's arm and pulled herself back onto the asphalt.

We continued the lesson, discussing the actions I used to show asphalt, rocks, a muddy slope, and the knee-high grass that lined the road. I revisit this technique in conferences, encouraging writers to *see* places as characters see them. I helped Jessica and Olivia step into Sherry's shoes, see out of her eyes, hear out of her ears, drawing on their experience playing in parks to construct the setting for the opening scene of "Why Did You Leave:" Our conference unfolded like this:

MS. J: You start your story saying "The girl was sitting in the park with her stepmom, two sisters, and one brother." I have trouble seeing this. I think you could strengthen the lead by describing the park a little bit, like your characters see it. Who's the most important character this scene?

JESSICA: The little girl.

MS. J: Look out of her eyes. When you say, "she was sitting in the park," what does she see as she looks around?

JESSICA: Well, there's this green bench she's on, kind of like the ones at Washington Park. And her brother's over in the sandbox. She's on the bench next to the sand.

OLIVIA: It's by the water and the water's under the bridge. There's a house in the back. Their house.

MS. J: So she's in a park near her house. Can she see her house?

JESSICA: Yes, it's sort of over the fence, behind the bench.

MS. J: Does she hear anything?

JESSICA: . . . some birds maybe and kids playing.

MS. J: I'm beginning to picture this. What kind of a day is it? Does it feel cold
to her, or hot. . . .

JESSICA: Hot . . . sunny.

OLIVIA: I was going to say it was a dark day.

JESSICA: Yeah, it could start raining.

MS. J: How does the little girl feel on this dark, rainy day?

JESSICA: She's sad.

OLIVIA: What I think is that it should be a gloomy day because it's like when
the sky is blue at first, and then it gets dark. . . .

JESSICA: Yeah, the clouds could go in front of the sun.

Several workshops later the girls completed a rewrite, incorporating
the "gloomy day," the "green bench," and the "sandbox" into the lead.
When I read this I felt a little disappointed that they added so little but
knew our talking helped them retrieve these new details, strengthening
the story.

Some writers need visuals to picture places—illustrations that encourage them to see colors, textures, shapes, relationships, and sizes. A quick
setting sketch—either pictorial or bird's-eye view—works well for most students. I used this strategy with Linda and Hien, both English Language
Learners, when we discussed "Brightstar and Mina" in late September. Several days prior to our talk Linda produced a cover and five scene sketches
and Hien wrote the following draft:

One day a dog named Brightstar was walking in the wood. She saw
a bird. She got hurt by a fox, so Brightstar chased the fox away. And
when she came back she took a piece of a leaf and she wrapped it
on the bird's stomach and she said, "Thanks, are you OK? What is
your name?" "Mina," said the bird. "My name is Brightstar."

So later on they went to Brightstar's house in the wood. It was
peaceful. Brightstar said to Mina, "Where is your family?" "They all
died." "Oh, I'm sorry to hear that," said Brightstar, "If there [is]
anything that I could help you with, I'll try.

So one day Mina said, "Let's go for a walk." "OK," said Brightstar. When they went to the woods the fox scared us from the
bushes. Then the fox ran because he's scared of Brightstar. Then
Brightstar said, "Let's have a picnic here." And Mina said, "OK." So
they went back to Brightstar's house and packed up food and pie
and juice. Brightstar said, "Let's go."

So Mina and Brightstar went to the woods. They put the sheet
on the grass and took out the food and pie and juices and they

ate. When they were done eating they played tag. When they were tired, they laid [*sic*] down on the grass. Brightstar and Mina lay there until the stars come [*sic*] out. Then Mina sang a song and Brightstar said, "That's nice." Then Brightstar and Mina fell asleep.

When it was morning, Mina was gone. "Oh, Oh, must be the fox." Then she heard "Help, help, help." "Oh, no. There's that dog again." Then the fox ran away. Then they lived happily ever after.

The story is about a friendship, much like their own. The place schema is simple: the action alternates between the relative danger of the woods and the

FIG. 5–1: Linda's "Tree Scene" for Brightstar and Mina

FIG. 5–2: Linda's "House Scene" for Brightstar and Mina

safety of Brightstar's house. In our first conference I asked about two of Linda's sketches, hoping to clarify the setting. Our conference began like this:

MS. J: Tell me about your first drawing.
LINDA: Mina got hurt, and she's taking a leaf to put around it.
MS. J: I see a tree in your picture. Is there a tree in your story?
LINDA: It's the woods. I drew it to show how she got hurt. I'm going to do it over again when we publish it.
MS. J: Why did you start your story in the woods?
LINDA: . . . because the fox lives in the woods and in the woods the fox could

catch the bird better. The woods was peaceful and nobody was there and it's easier for the fox to catch the bird.

HIEN: . . . and we wanted to do it right away so Mina could meet Brightstar right away.

MS. J: Do you picture anything else in this place?

LINDA: Lots of trees and its dark. I'm gonna put more trees. [long pause].

MS. J: Did you talk about this picture with Hien?

LINDA: No. But this is the woods, and I'm going to draw Brightstar's house because she brings her to her house to be unwounded [sic] so she could still fly by herself.

MS. J: Hien, are you going to put more in about the woods? [Hien shook her head indicating no.] I would like to picture this part better. I think it would help if you wrote more about it. When you think of the woods, what do you picture?

HIEN: There's a little tree, some kind of birds. [long pause]

MS. J: Have you ever been to the woods? [long pause]

HIEN: No . . . I don't think so.

MS. J: Have you ever seen a tree like the one in your picture?

LINDA: Well, it's like trees on both sides like this, there's a trail. Then when you walk through you see a path with lots of birds flying around and like there's one or two houses . . . like the houses are hiding so no one will know where they live . . . there are some snakes and . . . there's so many trees, like it's a hiding place and no one can see where you are at.

MS. J: Is this what you pictured, Hien? [Hien shrugged.] Linda, tell me what the trees look like.

LINDA: There like those. [She pointed out the window to a tree across the street from school.]

MS. J: Look at those trees, Hien. Do you think they should look like that? [Hien nodded yes] Linda, who lives in the houses?

LINDA: Mina lives in one and Brightstar lives in another. They're a few blocks away.

MS. J: So, how long would it take them to get to each other's houses? What do you think, Hien?

HIEN: I don't know, maybe ten blocks?

MS. J: How far away do you live from school?

LINDA: I live by a church. I don't know.

MS. J: Is it important how far apart their houses are in this story?

LINDA: No, because there's no . . . I'm not sure why.

MS. J: OK. Let's talk about Brightstar's house. What does it look like.

HIEN: Well, it's wood . . . with two windows.

LINDA: She has like a wooden place, right, like a Chinese house on the top. On the roof it has curls. On the bottom it's like there's a little door.

There's a little chimney. A window on the side of the door. The door is like, she doesn't have a key to her door. There's a secret hiding place . . . a mat under her door and when she opens the mat, there's the door and she sneaks in it.

MS. J: That's interesting. Let's read what you say about the house in your story. "Brightstar's house was bright as Brightstar." Who wrote that part?

Linda said that she wrote it.

What did you think Linda meant by that, Hien?

HIEN: It was bright, like yellowish.

MS. J: Linda, what were you picturing when you wrote this?

LINDA: The color was very bright . . . because the sunshine was shining very bright and in the rest of the woods there is no sunshine because the trees were covering it. It's like, also like painted bright colors. Light blue, yellow, and pink. And it was bright, like Brightstar's name.

Linda, the illustrator, had a much better sense of the "woods" and Brightstar's house than Hien. Like most collaborators, they constructed the piece without talking about setting. I wanted them to share ideas before our next conference, so I gave them a large sheet of paper to create another sketch, this time a bird's-eye view to map places in the story. They worked most of the morning, talking as they drew:

LINDA: That's there. Don't put that tree there.

HIEN: I don't get it.

LINDA: Just make everything small because the woods is BIG and, like the trees could be about that small, OK. Like . . .

HIEN: Is that where the bird will be?

LINDA: No, it's the pond. You don't need to draw the animals, just the trees.

HIEN: Aren't we going to draw the birds?

LINDA: No, later we have to draw Brightstar's house because that's where Mina was wounded.

HIEN: Flowers that we saw near the pond?

LINDA: OK. But we need trees, lots of trees.

Linda was clearly in charge, having a better visual sense of the story than Hien. Later on, Linda got another piece of paper, saying they "messed up. The tree is supposed to be in one place, and the pond, it's supposed to be far, and the river, it's supposed not to be too close to the pond." At one point Hien got frustrated and asked Linda where to put the tree where Brightstar found Mina. Linda said, "Just make sure it is very far from the pond." They also discussed how far the river was from the pond. Linda said it was "close." Hien responded that "you could see it." Linda made

FIG. 5–3: Linda and Hien's Setting Map

Brightstar's house "four levels. Brightstar lives in a big house. This is a mansion for her." Hien followed Linda's lead and made a "one-floor" house for Mina. With Linda's permission, Hien added flowers and "some roses." I talked to them shortly after they finished drawing, using the sketch to help us picture the opening scene:

MS. J: Now that you've mapped and talked about the woods, let's think about your lead: It goes, "One day a dog named Brightstar was walking in the woods." Show me on your map where they are right now. [Linda pointed to the area with trees.] What does it look like?

LINDA: That there are trees and birds.

MS. J: Describe it for me.

LINDA: Oh, it's like this place. We went to this place where we biked. I don't remember the name. It had mountains and grass and trees and birds.

MS. J: Last time we talked, Hien, you said you'd never been to the woods.

HIEN: Well, the class went to Audubon Canyon.

MS. J: What did that look like?

HIEN: Well, it had rivers and rocks. Little rocks that the water went over and little things . . .

LINDA: Newts!

HIEN: Yeah, and trees, redwood trees, pine trees, tall trees . . . and grasses, lots of birds and spiders.

MS. J: Can you picture the woods in your story like that?

LINDA: Yes.

HIEN: I think so.

MS. J: What could you add to your lead?

LINDA: I could put a river and a pond and birds.

A reminder Post-it said, "Look through Brightstar's eyes and describe the woods." The next day they changed the lead to read, "One day a dog named Brightstar was walking in the woods and there was [*sic*] rivers, pond, nest, trees, and a dog and the dog saw a bird." I should have anticipated this one. The description of the woods I carefully elicited turned into an attribute list. I assumed they remembered my earlier lessons, but like so many young writers, Linda and Hien needed support integrating new ideas into the text. Consequently, in our next conference, I reviewed one of the techniques I had previously demonstrated to help them rethink this part of the story:

MS. J: Can Brightstar see the river?

LINDA: Yes, it's close.

MS. J: How about the pond?

LINDA: She drinks water from the pond. There's a beach.

MS. J: . . . and where is Mina?

LINDA: She's hurt by the tree.

MS. J: Is she far from the pond?

LINDA: No, close. She's between the pond and the river.

MS. J: How does Brightstar see her?

LINDA: She looks up and sees her.

MS. J: What you've done so far is list the things we've talked about. You say, "There was rivers, pond, birds, nests . . . ," but it would be more interesting if you told us about the pond by having Brightstar *do* something. Do you remember how I added new details to my Tahiti story?

HIEN: The girl falls into the ditch?

MS. J: I wanted to show the ditch. It was completely dark and I made Rachel slip down the muddy slope. I showed the ditch by making her do something. What could your character do to show the pond?

LINDA: She could go to it.

HIEN: She could walk.

MS. J: She could do that . . . maybe take a drink of water.

We talked about other possibilities before Linda and Hien went back to their table to work on the opening again. They struggled for a day or two and finally replaced the list of descriptors with "One day a dog named Brightstar was walking in the woods. Brightstar could see the river and she was taking a drink from the pond. When she was done, she walked to this tree and took a nap." The image of the dog seeing the river and drinking water from the pond gives the lead a much better sense of place and sets the mood for the story. Our picture of the woods is strengthened when the characters revisit the pond for a picnic on the grass. The girls' final draft reads like this:

> One day a dog named Brightstar was walking in the woods. She could see the river. She took a drink from the pond. When she was done, she walked to the tree and went to take a nap. She went to the tree, and she saw a bird. The bird got hurt by the fox. Brightstar chased the fox away. And when she came back she took a piece of a leaf and she wrapped it on the bird's stomach. The bird said, "Thank you." "Are you OK?" said Brightstar, "What is your name?" "Mina," said the bird.
>
> Later on they went to Brightstar's house in the woods. It was peaceful. Brightstar said to Mina, "Where is your family?" "They all died by the fox." "Oh, I'm sorry to hear that, " said Brightstar. "If there is anything that I could help you with, I'll try." One day Mina said, "Let's go for a walk." "OK," said Brightstar.

When they went to the woods, the fox scared Brightstar and Mina from the bushes. The fox ran because he's scared of Brightstar. Then Brightstar said, "Let's have a picnic." Mina said, "OK." They went back to Brightstar's house and packed up food and drinks.

"Let's go to the pond," and Brightstar and Mina went to the woods. They put the sheet on the grass and took out the food and drinks and they ate. When they were done eating, then they played tag. When they were tired, they laid [*sic*] down on the grass. Brightstar and Mina lay there until the stars came out. Mina sang a song and Brightstar said, " That's nice." Brightstar and Mina fell asleep.

When it was morning, Mina was gone! "Oh, no! I think she's been kidnapped by the fox!" She heard a voice. It said, "Help, help!" Brightstar said, "I think it is her." She ran to look for Mina. She barked, "Woof, woof! I gave you the first warning. I'm not going to give you the second one!" The dog bit the fox until she bled. The fox ran away and they lived happily ever after.

Researching Settings

Linda and Hien used memories of Audubon Canyon to construct a make-believe forest, but sometimes writers have to stretch their imaginations, synthesizing new information to create unfamiliar settings. When Ricky wrote "War with My Uncle," he set the story in colonial Massachusetts, a place he knew only from illustrations in *Sam the Minuteman* (Benchley 1987). It was difficult for him to picture the setting, so I asked him to refer to the illustrations in *Sam* and sketch the house, the road, and other places described in his first draft. We talked about the sketch in a follow-up conference the next day:

MS. J: Tell me about your sketch..

RICKY: There's, like, brick walls here that they could duck under, kind of. I got that from *Sam the Minuteman*. They were, like, hiding behind a tree and a brick wall. And this is a bridge here. It's kind of curvedlike with brick. And then there's walls, and this is grass. It's like two houses every . . . mile . . . like two right here.

MS. J: Why only two houses?

RICKY: Well, the Minutemen were a very small group. There was [*sic*] like, five houses over here.

MS. J: That makes sense because very few people lived in Massachusetts then.

RICKY: I got that from the book.

FIG. 5–4: Ricky's Setting Map

MS. J: Why don't you draw the Minutemen and the British?

[Ricky drew the figures.]

RICKY: These are some of the Minutemen. They're on the road. They are trying to shoot these people out. These are the British and they are burning
down this house, like, one of the fighter's houses. And this is a bridge
and more British come to fight.

MS. J: You say that they hide behind walls [*pointed to sketch*]. What do the
walls look like?

RICKY: I think they're red and chipped . . . sort of white, like cement on them.

MS. J: And Thomas' house? Do you picture it?

RICKY: A little bit. I'm not sure.

At this point, I took Ricky to the history library to browse through a book containing photographs of extant New England colonial architecture (Mullins 1987). We turned the pages, noting the neat rows of rectangular windows and Ionic porch columns that distinguish these simple, boxy houses. Ricky selected a house for his characters, and we returned with the book to his table to resume our conversation. I wanted him to continue thinking about setting, this time placing himself in the shoes of his main character to flesh out the action:

MS. J: When you say, "The British walked back toward Boston," let's try to see this through your character's eyes. Put yourself in your map. Thomas is here. He drags his dad into the house, a house just like this one. [*I pointed to the photograph.*] How does he know the "British walked back to Boston?" What does he see or hear?

RICKY: He hears them leaving, like walking away, like walking back.

MS. J: What does he hear?

RICKY: Well, they say, "Go back."

MS. J: Who says this?

RICKY: The commander. He'll say, like, "We'll come back later."

MS. J: How close are they to the house?

RICKY: This is the house. This is the bridge. This is when they are, like, hiding. When the British leave they are, like, hiding here [*he pointed to the tree near the house*] and trying not to get shot.

MS. J: I don't see the Dad or the boy. Could you draw them in? [Ricky drew figures on the map.] OK, how far away are the British when the dad gets shot?

RICKY: Pretty close, about ten yards.

MS. J: When you say "he looks back," where does he look?

RICKY: When his dad gets shot he looks back here [*he pointed to place near "British house"*] to see who shot him, across the road.

MS. J: And what does he see?

RICKY: He saw the British on the other side of the wall.

MS. J: When you say "leaving," what do you mean?

RICKY: They started running back to the city.

MS. J: How does Thomas know they are going to Boston?

RICKY: I don't know.

MS. J: Well, if you are seeing this through your character's eyes, he will see them leaving but may not know where they are going. What does he see as they are leaving?

RICKY: They run back over the bridge.
MS. J: Picture it like you did on your map. How do they leave?
RICKY: He saw them climbing over the wall and running over the bridge.

Ricky came to the conference with a sketch; during our talk I asked him to draw the characters, providing a visual aid to help him think through the action in this scene. He began to picture the colonial countryside during the course of our conversation, incorporating his new understanding into the lead of his final draft:

> Boom! Thomas looked at his dad. He was shot. Thomas looked back across the road. He saw a big red line of British soldiers on the other side of the brick wall. "That's who shot him," Thomas said. He dragged his dad inside their house.
>   Thomas saw out his front window, the British jumping over the wall and heading toward the woods. His mom patched his dad up. Thomas talked to his mom about the war. The Minutemen were losing. "I hope I do not shoot my uncle," Thomas said, "You know he is on the British side."

The books and the sketch helped Ricky picture rural Massachusetts in the 1770s. He learned about brick-walled roads and boxy colonial houses scattered among woods and clearings. In this process he learned something else: as he began to visualize the setting he also clarified the plot, vicariously living the events in the story as he moved from place to place, running, crying, looking out the living room window, listening to the sound of British gunfire.

CLARIFYING PLOT

Ricky discovered what all good fiction writers know: effective settings are intimately related to plot because "what happens to the character could happen in the way it happens only in that particular setting" (Jason and Lefcowitz 1990, 178). Although plot is not simply the sum of *what happens*, actions are "the most visible elements of plot," the way the reader sees "what the writer has prepared . . . a conflict with complications . . . a crisis . . . and a resolution" (175). Plot is a scheme to reveal characters, a set of interrelated actions organized by the writer and driven by the logic of the actors who inhabit a fictional world.

Kids don't understand these subtleties, but they understand action. They know how to create connected events that make sense, events that mirror their own lives and the lives of the characters they see on TV, and in books, movies, and video games. However, they often run into difficulty constructing logical, well-shaped story lines, even though this is the easiest element of fiction for them to master. Plot difficulties revolve around three issues: getting stuck, plot logic, and shaping the story. We address these problems as they occur, reflecting on demonstration lessons, researching missing information, drawing, sequencing events, and talking about plot in conferences and in small- and whole-group shares.

Getting Unstuck

Most young writers discover stories by "writing along until the direction reveals itself, almost like magic" (Jason and Lefcowitz 1990, 174). Less often they "start with a character and invent situations . . . or start with a plot and invent characters" (176). Getting stuck midstory happens often because, as Nanci Atwell (1998) suggests, ten-year-olds try to "draft and craft" at the same time. Stepping away from the act of constructing and recording sentences allows them to disentangle story from storytelling and refocus on plot discovery. Brainstorming in peer shares helps because it allows writers to relax and play with new ideas. Jessica and Olivia asked Lori and Sandy to help with "Why Did You Leave" when they couldn't figure out how to explain why the father kills himself and the mother ends up hating the daughter:

LORI: I think you should have a scary part when the mom was going to kill her stepdaughter.

SANDY: I have a lot of suggestions for that one.

JESSICA: I don't like that. It's too violent.

SANDY: You could have it one night, dark, and her mom sneaked into her room and stabbed her with a knife.

LORI: Yeah, stabbed her with a knife and then her spirit comes back and haunts her mom and she gets freaked out and she dies.

JESSICA: We don't want to make it so complicated.

SANDY: Wait, wait. My idea was that you write one night her mom just killed her because she was sick of her daughter. She wanted to kill her because she hated her father and they have a fight one night. And they want to hit each other. They hate each other. They're hitting each other. Her mom gets a knife and she tries to kill her but she doesn't kill her but they have this big old fight. But that's not your story.

OLIVIA: How about this? If they were poor people and the dad died because he was mad at himself . . .

JESSICA: . . . they wouldn't have any money.

OLIVIA: Yeah, they don't have enough money because the dad died and he felt sad that he always hit his daughter. Then his spirit comes back and he gives the daughter whatever she wants and then she turns rich and everything but then they find out that living rich is nothing, so they want to be poor and they suffer from stuff, from being rich, like all those reporters come and they, like . . .

JESSICA: Like, the rich is poor and the poor is rich.

SANDY: The rich is poor because they have a bad life and . . .

LORI: So the spirit comes back and gives her everything.

JESSICA: We think the first story is better. When the father was always hitting the daughter she felt like hitting him back, right.

SANDY: Maybe one time the daughter can hit him back, one time. Like, first you have, OK, I have a whole new story. First the dad is alive, right? and then you say, "Oh, my dad always hit me all the time." And then one day you could tell about him hitting her and the girl hitting him back and then he'll say, "Oh, my God, I hit my child!" Then he knows how it feels so he could go out and . . .

JESSICA: . . . and kills himself.

SANDY: Exactly! He goes out in the car—wherever he's going—and kills himself!

In this freewheeling discussion, the girls excitedly argued over possible plot solutions, weighing suggestions and piggybacking ideas. Lori and Sandy suggested violence; Jessica rejected it. Olivia created another scenario; Sandy listened and modified her ideas, and finally Jessica and Sandy agreed that the father kills himself because he feels guilty about hitting his daughter. This unfocused session led to a solution the authors adopted the next day as they continued to write.

I step in when peer shares like this don't work, when the group gets silly or stuck or both. Sometimes I suggest that writers list possibilities on a separate sheet of paper before we talk; at other times a quick conference seems to move the story along. If neither approach works, I encourage authors to set the piece aside for a while and start something new. Ricky retrieved "War Against My Uncle" from his storage folder after getting stuck on the plot for several weeks. He didn't know what to do after introducing his young revolutionary hero in the lead to the first draft. The father and son are on their way to New Hampshire to buy a rifle , and Ricky wants to get them back to the house in time for a skirmish with the British. He worried that it would "take too long" and discussed the problem with Eric, who told him to "just say it." Ricky wasn't sure how to "say it," so he came to me for a conference hoping to "figure out what's next." In our talk we identified the central story conflict, evaluated whether the trip should be added to the piece, and decided to open the story with a battle set in the front yard of the house.

Searching for Plot Logic

Young writers often scramble story lines as they rush headlong into the piece, creating gaps and illogical events that leave the reader perplexed and disconcerted. Kids are impatient writers who fill stories with actions that belie feelings, contradict common sense, or show the writer's youthful knowledge of the world. We begin identifying illogical events in demonstrations and whole-group shares early in the year. By March or April I often overhear writers say "that part doesn't make sense," questioning the rationale behind a behavior, the reason behind an event, the mysterious appearance of a new setting. These challenges encourage authors to slow down, rethink the story, and "connect the characters to our world in a logical way" (Jason and Lefcowitz 1990, 175).

I help the process along in lessons where we imagine what we would do if we were in a character's shoes. Sometimes we stop in the middle of a novel, recap events, and predict what will happen next. Are our predictions consistent with the feelings and behavior of the character and what we know about the world? Will Alyce, after awakening on the side of the road in *The Midwife's Apprentice,* return to the village she left in humiliation or continue down the path to some unknown place (Cushman 1995, 73)? What subsequent action makes sense?

I encourage authors to ponder similar questions in student–teacher conferences. In Susan's "Map" story, I questioned how she constructed the "note scene," helping her see that her protagonist's response is inconsistent with previous story events and the way she might act if she were in the same situation:

MS. J: You say that "Susan picked up the envelope and put it in her pocket." This doesn't make sense to me. What just happened in the classroom?

SUSAN: Kids disappear in the map.

MS. J: And how does Susan feel about that?

SUSAN: Probably, like, . . . scared and "I hope it was a dream."

MS. J: How does she feel when she turns the doorknob?

SUSAN: Uh, maybe "I hope no one is there."

MS. J: Does it make sense, then, that she would just pick up the note and put it in her pocket? I mean, it seems she would act this way if it were a normal day, but not after what just happened in class.

SUSAN: Well, maybe she goes slow to the door. "Susan slowly walked to the door, thinking it was a dream."

MS. J: . . . or "wondering if it were a dream" to show that she's not sure if it is or not. This would help explain her actions to the reader.

In this conference I focused Susan's attention on two movements, turning the knob and seeing the note. I wanted her to feel what her character feels as she responds to the knock at the door. This simple conversation helped her rethink, but others need visuals, especially when they're confused about the story in the first place. I often ask these students to make a setting sketch and superimpose actions, reconstructing events scene by scene by using stick figures and arrows to show how characters move from place to place. Ricky did this to clarify "War." Mary created a similar sketch for "Monsters, Monsters Everywhere" after other writers told her that they "don't have a clue what's happening after (the character) sits down." Mary didn't know either: In her story a girl comes home from school, sees a mysterious pair of eyes, and runs through the house and out the back door chased by a series of monsters. We discussed her sketch in the following conference:

Mary read the story:

Jessica was eating the rest of her lunch while waiting for her mom to show up at school. She waited and waited until she just could not wait any longer and she started to walk home. By the time she got home, she saw that the door was open and she walked right in. The house was dark and she didn't want to turn on the lights because she was scared that something would happen. All of a sudden, she felt something soft and furry rubbing on her leg. She looked down. It was her cat, Emerald. "So, you're the only one here," she said. She thought her friends were coming to her sleepover and said to herself, "I guess they're not coming to my birthday sleepover after all," and went in the living room and picked up the remote and turned on the TV. Suddenly she heard a low, loud growl. She heard the basement door close and she looked up. She saw red eyes, yellow eyes, and green eyes. She ran. A monster appeared. She ran again. Another monster appeared. She ran everywhere, but everywhere she ran, a monster appeared. She ran to the backyard and shut the sliding glass door. The grass started breaking and monsters were coming out of the grass. "AHHHHHHHHHH!" "Happy birthday!" said all the monsters taking off their masks.

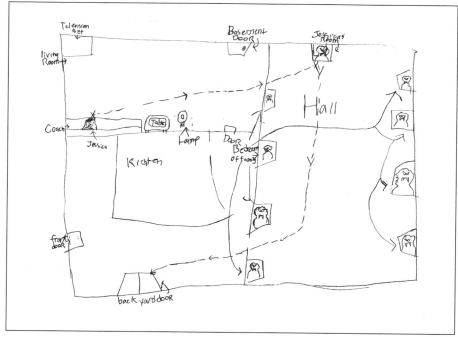

FIG. 5–5: Mary's Action Map

MS. J: I like the first part of your story, right up to the part where you say, "She saw red eyes. . . ." I get confused after that. Show me where the action starts.

MARY: Right here. [*She pointed to the figure labeled "Jessica."*] She's on the couch, and she's watching TV until she hears this low growl, and she looks up and there's this pair of eyes in front of her.

MS. J: Where are the eyes?

MARY: Over here, above the TV.

MS. J: OK, then what happens?

MARY: Then she runs from the couch to here.

[*She pointed to a line that appeared to be the wall dividing the living room from the hall.*]

MS. J: What's over there?

MARY: The hall.

MS. J: Is there an opening or a door here?

MARY: [pause] That's an opening. And I put in the basement door here 'cause kids didn't know where that was when she hears the growl.

MS. J: When does she hear it?
MARY: When she's on the couch.
MS. J: Can she hear the growl from there?
MARY: Yeah . . . It's sort of close. . . .
MS. J: Where does she go after she's in the hallway?
MARY: To her room.

I use another activity to help authors see *jumps*, places in stories where characters move from one setting or action to another with no explanation or apparent reason. The year I wrote "What Did You Say?" I read the story and asked the class to fold paper into squares, and sequence, label, and draw the setting and action for each box. Then we reread the piece to analyze, scene by scene, whether I explained Susan and Linda's movements. We learned that I hadn't shown how they ended up on the basement stairs after a lengthy conversation in the bedroom. To show how to make an abrupt scene shift, I added, "They cautiously made their way down the hall to the basement door," explaining that I wanted to move the characters quickly, not spend too much time in transitions that detract from the narrative focus.

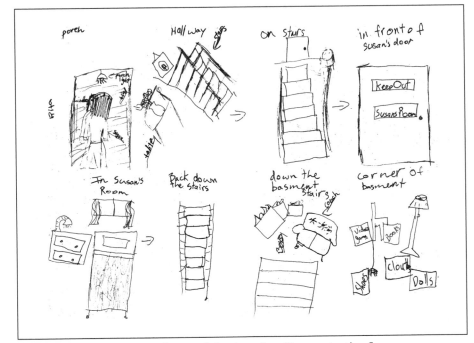

FIG. 5–6: Sequencing Actions and Settings in a Demonstration Lesson

After a while writers begin to find *jumps* on their own, and soon this becomes a focus for peer shares. We also discuss *jumps* in conferences. I asked James and Ricky to chart places and actions for "The Haunted Teachers." As we talked they realized that Steven, the main character, landed in the classroom without explanation. We discussed ways to handle the problem, and I suggested they move Steven by starting a new paragraph. They jotted the suggestion on a Post-it and returned to their table to write, "Steven felt nervous the next morning when he went to class."

I provide information or suggest additional research when writers lack the necessary knowledge to construct logical story lines. In Cindy's "Too Many Tears," Susan and her husband Joe go to the hospital and enter the Having Baby Room. Two hours later a nurse appears holding Joe's new offspring. Joe runs off to work, and Susan goes home only to return to the hospital after a two-week break because "her stomach hurts." She promptly produces a twin and brings the latest member of the family back to the house. Obviously, Cindy didn't know much about having babies, so talking to her about experiences wouldn't help unscramble this mess. She was not interested in researching the topic, so I gave her a few facts and she moved on with the story.

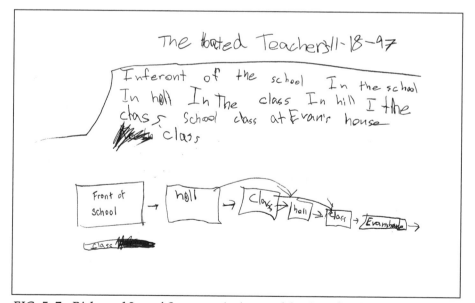

FIG. 5–7: *Ricky and James' Sequence Actions and Settings for* The Haunted Teachers

Sophia needed new information to sort out the logic of "A New Life in a New World." Sandy, the main character, "flies to Nigeria" in the 1850s to live in a village with her uncle. She "takes a shower in the bathroom" of her adopted family's "air conditioned" house. Sophia filled her first draft with anachronistic, ethnocentric events based on her experiences in Alameda, creating plot without understanding setting. She said the story is "about a girl who has a new life in a new world," just like her title. She wanted it to take place "a long time ago," so I suggested that she read about Africa before our next conference. A few days later we browsed through a book[2], gathering information to reconstruct the story as we talked:

SOPHIA: I think I want her to go to An . . . , Angola. It's on this page.
MS. J: Why do you like this place?
SOPHIA: I don't know; it just looks interesting.
MS. J: What do you notice in this illustration?
SOPHIA: The houses, like the hut things.
MS. J: What else?
SOPHIA: Different areas.
MS. J: What do you mean?
SOPHIA: A goat pen, or a meeting place, the second wife's house, her little area.
MS. J: What do you think they mean, "second wife?"
SOPHIA: I guess he has two wives.
MS. J: Sounds like it. What do you think these women are doing?
She pointed to a group of women grinding flour.
SOPHIA: I think that's where they grind the food.
MS. J: The caption says that it's "an enclosure for grinding a harvest of millet and sorghum." They grow it like we grow wheat and then grind it into flour to make bread and other food.

Sophia noticed the "children's hut"; the arid countryside; the stones, branches, hay, and mud brick used in the compound; the lack of electricity; and the dirt road. Could Sandy take a shower in a bathroom or fly on a plane? Sophia decided that Sandy sailed on the Queen of Angola as we continued talking about what happened to her character in this new setting:

SOPHIA: I think when she gets off the boat she sees it's different from California.
MS. J: Ships arrive at a dock, like the wharf here in Alameda. What does she see from the dock?
SOPHIA: She sees a village.

MS. J: Can she walk to the village or does she have to take a bus?

SOPHIA: She takes a bus and meets her uncle.

MS. J: So you might want to create a scene here, seeing and hearing like your character as she steps off the boat. Where's the bus?

SOPHIA: It's by the dock.

MS. J: So as she stands there she hears and sees?

SOPHIA: The bus.

MS. J: She hears the bus coming closer and closer. She rides the bus to the village and someone meets her. What does her uncle do?

SOPHIA: He's a farmer.

MS. J: Does he greet her as she gets off the bus?

SOPHIA: Yes, and her cousins and aunts.

MS. J: The uncle might be there, but if he's a farmer and she arrives in the middle of the day, he could still be working. You just need to think about these things, about what people might do in Angola, as you decide what your characters do. Also, remember to give us lots of detail—like describing what she sees in the village—so when Sandy does something it seems like she is in Africa a long time ago and not in Alameda today.

I helped Sophia think through the logic of her character's actions, the logic of events that unfold as Sandy moves from the dock to the bus to the village. Later, we talked one more time, focusing attention on her character's feelings as she explored this strange, new land. I left the conference wondering if Sophia would integrate these new ideas into the piece. Over the next week she revised her story several times. In her final draft Sandy sailed to Africa with a map to her uncle's village, an idea she developed during our second conversation. These changes helped bring plot and setting closer together. She wrote:

> After she arrived, she stepped out on the dock and what she saw was much different than what California looked like. In a distance, she could see a small city and while she stared at the city, she heard a sound, and it got louder. Then she turned around and saw a bus that lead [*sic*] to her uncle's village far away from the dock. She got on the bus and sat next to a window. The bus started up and away they went.
>
> Sandy looked out the window as she entered the city. The bus ride was a long bus ride. Finally, the bus ride was over, and she got out and looked at her map. Sandy picked up her bags and off she went to her uncle's village. When she was there, she made sure she was in the right place. She saw that the village had different houses.

She noticed that over the fence a woman was grinding beans. She heard the crack, crack, crack sound of the beans. She saw goats, and the people's meeting house, a guest house, and some empty pens for the goats.

She walked looking for her uncle's hut made of wood, hay, and mud bricks. She thought how it would be to live in a new country. Where was her uncle? Suddenly she bumped into a girl with fruit in a basket on her head. This was strange. She never saw a person carry a basket of fruit on their head before.

"Hey, watch where you are going!" Sandy yelled.

"I brought some fruit. I thought you would be hungry. We are cousins. I've come to show you to your hut. Actually, we share it with my dad. Let's go unpack your things. Then we will go and look at the village."

I worked with Sophia to align plot and setting, bringing logic to the sequence of action in her story. We also did something else: we rebuilt the plot, reconstructed events to explore her story premise: a girl adapts to life in a new land. We created a new series of events to develop her original idea, her "picture about which the story had yet to be told and put that situation in motion" (Jason and Lefcowitz 1990, 176).

Like Sophia, many young writers create an interesting premise but lack the skill to construct the plot, especially when the situation is complex or outside their experience. A story idea as simple as Mustafa's "cat chases rat looking for cheese" in "Garry and Matt" presents fewer plot dilemmas than Sophia's "New World" or Susan's "kids disappear into a school map." When writers take on too much, I validate the story idea but suggest they redo the storytelling. We identify the premise, scrap the plot, and begin again, thinking through the piece event by event.

However, writers lose energy if they struggle with a story too long, when they discover that the premise doesn't make sense or it's too complex for them to handle or they need too much new information to make it work. In these cases I suggest they abandon the piece if they haven't decided to do so already. This happened to Susan's "Map" story, a piece she wrote off and on for two months. She created a complex story situation, and multiple responses from other writers added to her confusion as she attempted to construct the plot. Kids questioned details—how does the teacher hide the microphone or keep students in their seats while others disappear? Some wondered why the teacher and the janitor wanted to kill the kids in the first place. Susan experimented with ways to solve these problems but decided to set the story aside because it became "too weird":

SUSAN: I screwed it up.

MS. J: What do you mean?

SUSAN: I just wanted to have a letter that tells, like, how they can find the teacher and try to save the kids. I messed it up. I wrote a letter and Susan is reading it and it's not really focused now.

MS. J: Why isn't it focused?

SUSAN: I don't know. It's just weird. I think (the reader) is going to get confused here 'cause the letter is trying to tell them why they put the kids in the map. I say "Dear Roboto"—that's the teacher—but I don't want to tell them that it's really a robot that's acting like the teacher and she's really in the janitor's closet. And you know that other part, the way they take them out of the map? I haven't figured it out yet. But see, that's the whole plan. The dead ones, they just hide somewhere but the live ones (the teacher and the janitor) find them, and they're heroes and they get, like, money.

MS. J: I'm still confused. Are the kids that come out of the map going to know what happens?

SUSAN: I don't know.

I suggested that she think about this but sensed she was fatigued, tired of struggling with so many complex plot issues. We both felt relief when she abandoned the story right after returning from winter break. She told me that she "couldn't figure out how to solve all the problems, like how to get Susan to find out about the janitor . . . and about the kids being dead and nobody cares. It got too weird, and I didn't want to work on it."

Susan abandoned her piece but extended her understanding of fiction as she struggled to create the complicated web of events necessary to tell her story. She pushed herself, evaluated cause and effect, weighed alternative sequences of events, pondered connections between feelings and actions, attempting to put this complex tale together. I pushed her as far as I could, monitoring her reactions as I challenged her to take her thinking to a new level, just short of frustration but within her capacity to grow as a thinker and as a writer.

Shaping the Story

A central problem drives the plot in Susan's "Map": how to rescue disappearing classmates. Susan created tension and mystery as her young, self-appointed detective discovers notes, overhears talk on a hidden microphone, and ponders the strange actions of her teacher and the janitor.

Susan constructed what some ten-year-olds can't: a dramatic plot with a conflict for the characters to resolve. There's no such tension in the stories many young fifth-graders write. They create *bed-to-bed* fiction that resembles bed-to-bed personal narrative: shapeless, unfocused pieces lacking what Leland (1998, 124) calls the structure of a traditional story, "a central figure, . . . who has a desire and a sequence of events that leads him to overcome—or not—the realization of that desire."

When I shape fiction with writers, we work to discover the conflict, climax, and resolution hidden in flat-line narratives, taking Rebecca Rule's advice and "concentrating on the main character because something will happen . . . a conflict will erupt in a crisis, and your story will have a plot" (Rule and Wheeler 1993, 96). We identify interesting events, search for focus, and build drama by imagining how characters feel in different story situations.

I used this technique to help Ronnie focus "Wrong Exit," a story based on a real-life trip to the NBA Jam at the Oakland Coliseum. The piece opens with a neighbor's invitation. Ronnie then chronicles the rest of the day, including taking a wrong turn, getting lost, finding the Coliseum, watching the competition, and returning home in the evening to "eat dinner." Ronnie discovered three possible story problems as we talked. We discussed each one, deciding that the "wrong exit" problem presented the greatest potential for vitality and drama.

In a similar fashion I helped James shape "What Was That," another fictionalized personal narrative lacking focus and dramatic tension. The story goes like this: three kids stay home while their parents "go somewhere." Peter, the main character, investigates several mysterious sounds, walking from room to room until his parents come home and tell him they "had a good time." In our conference James said he liked the scene when the boy hears the first noise and the ending when the parents walk in the door. He identified the noises as the story problem, and I suggested that the parents bring something home to solve the mystery. The next day we discussed what Peter hears, sees, and feels in the first scene and, later, as he moves through the house. Over several weeks James rewrote the story, adding details showing Peter "tiptoeing" down the hall, "looking through the door mailbox," and searching behind closet doors to discover the source of the sounds. With the help of another writer James identified a popping tire as one source and ended the piece identifying the other when the parents came home to tell him that a noisy new "baby Labrador Retriever" was on the back porch.

Other young writers struggle with endings, not knowing how to resolve a conflict at the close of a story. Jacob and Steven suggested to Ricky that the British blow up the house in the final scene of "War," but Ricky wasn't sure he wanted to finish things that way. In his first attempt he brings the wounded uncle into the house, writing "Finally, they let him go because he was their uncle." In our conference I focused his attention on the main character, hoping he would devise an ending that resolved the boy's conflict over the accidental shooting:

MS. J: I think you need to resolve Thomas feelings at the end of the story. How does he feel when he sees his uncle in this last scene?
RICKY: Kind of scared because he is yelling at him and stuff.
MS. J: How about some dialogue between Thomas and the uncle? Or you could let us know how Thomas feels by telling us his thoughts.
RICKY: Like, he could say, "I can't believe you shot me, you little kid."
MS. J: And Thomas responds?
RICKY: He says, like whispers, he mumbles, "I wish this war never happened."

Ricky added his new ending that morning, completing "War" after weeks of thoughtful revision. In the process he learned how to see out of his characters' eyes, connecting actions to feelings as he constructed the plot and, finally, turned to his characters to bring his story to a satisfying close.

DISCOVERING THEMES, EVALUATING CRAFT

Sandy explored the consequences of competition in her basketball story, "Too Tall for Jenny." Ricky examined compassion, ambivalence, and the moral dilemmas posed by revolution as he wrote "War Against My Uncle." The meaning of these stories emerges as characters interact and struggle to resolve the central story conflict. Like most writers, kids construct implicit themes in stories, embedding messages about good and evil, relationships, strivings, courage, fears, and remorse. We write to explore what it is to be human, and every story "raises questions, examines possibilities, and imagines the consequences of actions" (Stern 1991, 241). Themes come about because characters drive fiction and, as Leland (1998) suggests, "emerge as the writer's voice emerges" (140–41).

However, kids don't see the "so what" (Rule and Wheeler 1993, 209) in their tales—the abstractions generalized from particular events and actions. Unlike adult writers, they operate on a concrete, literal level, unable to begin with a theme or discover it as they work through the story, pondering "small pieces of information, seeing their significance as [they] go along, and write to discover what these details add up to" (Rule and Wheeler, 107). Thus, they need our help to find the meaning that comes "bubbling up out of [their] unconscious and onto the page" (Leland, 140).

I help young writers explore themes in conferences and in lessons by taking Rebecca Rule's advice: we "go back to the first line and explore [the] character deeply" (210). In both discussions I focus on how characters approach problems and the lessons they learn by interacting with others in the story. Then we discuss what we learn as outsiders, as eavesdroppers, watching the drama unfold. Kids are pretty good at this, especially after weeks of exploring characters on their own and with other writers.

When I conferred with Ronnie about "Off Road Race," we discussed his characters' reactions after the race is over, focusing on how they attempt to solve the central story conflict:

MS. J: So who wins the race?

RONNIE: Ronnie does. Paulo gets his car in the water and then he gets it out but he loses.

MS. J: How does he feel about that?

RONNIE: He wants a rematch.

MS. J: Ah, that's the way your story ends. How does Ronnie feel about what Paulo says?

RONNIE: He's sad.

MS. J: Why?

RONNIE: Because Paulo's a sore loser.

MS. J: And they're friends, right?

RONNIE: Yeah.

MS. J: And Ronnie learns that his friend is . . .

RONNIE: . . . a bad sport.

MS. J: What do we learn from watching them?

RONNIE: Maybe that you shouldn't be a sore loser because your friends might get mad at you.

I helped Ronnie abstract meaning by reviewing the actions and motivations of his characters. In a similar manner, Marissa discovered that Jennifer in "The Wind Sounds Like My Cry" learns to deal with teasing, teaching us that "sometimes you can face your fears and it's OK." Jessica believed that Sherry in "Why Did You Leave" finally decides that "it isn't her fault that her dad died." Ricky said "War Against My Uncle" shows that "there shouldn't be wars because you can kill someone you know or your own family like Thomas did." These authors discovered meaning when they stepped away from the act of writing to reflect, looking carefully at the fictional world they and their characters created.

Discovering meaning is half of the process: analyzing the craft of storytelling is the other. We evaluate craft all year long, "thoughtfully assessing and reassessing what [we] write" (Gardiner 1984, 9). We look at leads, endings, shape, scenes, characterization, setting, and logic, examining what we do and how we grow. After a writer completes a story, I ask: What do you think of your piece? Where did you get stuck and what did you do to solve the problem? What do you like best? Why do you like that part? What would you change if you could? How does this piece compare with other stories you've written?

Some writers are more reflective than others. Tony thought that "it doesn't make sense that kids go in a camp when no one's there" but didn't want to change "Camp Horror." Patrick learned that writing fiction is "really hard and confusing." He still believed he had "too much talking" in "Hurry Up" and said he'd put in a bike scene if he had another go at it. Jacob was satisfied with "Evil J II" and liked it better than "Evil J I" because it contained "more description and that really good part when Patrick falls out of the window." Susan maintained that "Map" "got all stupid" but she "liked the idea of it, that kids could disappear like that." She said she might try it again next year, but right now it's "too boring." Steven abandoned "Ruff, Ruff" and, like Susan, thought he "had a good idea to start out with." He told me that he "just lost hope in it because Jacob got mad when (he) named the dog after him." He felt better after Ricky borrowed the premise and wrote "Dognapped." Ricky said his characters in "War" seemed real because they "show their feelings like when the Dad gets mad at Thomas for shooting his uncle, and Thomas mumbles because he's upset." Lori thought her lead character in "Bathtub" was believable, too, because she "acts and feels like real people do." Sophia remarked that she liked the closet scene in "Fairytale Island" because she saw it through her character's eyes, and "it had its own meaning and seemed so clear to me." She wanted to add details from her drawing to "show the rainbows and the grass," but she ran out of time and "Marissa told me to keep it simple."

Images of writers working together, crafting characters, setting, and plot emerge from these interviews. Over the course of a year's workshop these authors learn to evaluate the people in their stories, questioning their intentions and the logic of their actions. They learn to draw from experience to construct settings other readers can picture and understand. They shape stories, know when a scene works, and see the meaning in their tales, the reason we write fiction at all. They create improved but imperfect pieces, learning to think and talk like writers.

NOTES

1. Many of the insights in this section are based on research conducted with Kira Walker and included in an unpublished manuscript entitled *A Child's Sense of Place: Exploring Places as Children Write Fiction* (1997). For more on how children construct landscapes and on spatial understanding, see M. H. Matthews, *Making Sense of Plalce: Children's Understanding of Large-scale Environments* (Savage, MD: Barnes and Noble Books, 1992); Christopher Spencer, *The Child and the Physical Environment: The Development of Spatial Knowledge and Cognition* (New York: Wiley, 1989).

2. *Africa: Eyewitness Books* (New York: Dorling Kingsley, 1995) p. 43.

Books About Writing

Anderson, Carl. 2000. *How's It Going? A Practical Guide to Conferencing with Student Writers*. Portsmouth, NH: Heinemann.

Atwell, Nanci. 1998. *In the Middle*. Portsmouth, NH: Heinemann.

———. 1990. *Coming to Know: Writing to Learn in the Intermediate Grades*. Portsmouth, NH: Heinemann.

Brusto, Mike. 1999. *Writing Rules*. Portsmouth, NH: Heinemann.

Burke, Carol and Tinsley, Molly Best. 1993. *The Creative Process*. New York: St. Martin's Press.

Burroway, Janet. 2000. *Writing Fiction: A Guide to Narrative Craft*. New York: Longman.

Caulkins, Lucy. 1986. *The Art of Teaching Writing*. Portsmouth, NH: Heinemann.

———. 1991. *Living Between the Lines*. Portsmouth, NH: Heinemann.

Chiarella, Tom. 1998. *Writing Dialogue*. Cincinnati: Story Press.

Clark, Roy Peter. 1995. *Free to Write*. Portsmouth, NH: Heinemann.

D'Arcy, Pat. 1989. *Making Sense, Making Meaning*. Portsmouth, NH: Boynton/Cook.

Dyson, Anne Haas. 1997. *Writing Superheroes: Contemporary Children, Modern Culture, and Classroom Literacy*. New York: Teachers College Press.

Gardiner, James. 1984. *The Art of Fiction*. New York: Alfred A. Knopf.

Graves, Donald. 1989. *Experiments with Fiction*. Portsmouth, NH: Heinemann.

———. 1994. *A Fresh Look at Writing*. Portsmouth, NH: Heinemann.

Graves, Richard. 1999. *Writing, Teaching, Learning*. Portsmouth, NH: Boynton/Cook.

Harste, Jerome, Kathy Short, and Carolyn Burke. 1988. *Creating Classrooms for Authors.* Portsmouth, NH: Heinemann.

Jason, Philip K., and Allan Lefcowitz. 1990. *Creative Writer's Handbook.* Englewood Cliffs, NJ: Prentice-Hall.

Leland, Christopher. 1998. *The Art of Compelling Fiction.* Cincinnati: Story Press.

Moffett, James. 1987. *Active Voice I: A Writer's Reader* (Grades 4–6). Portsmouth, NH: Boynton/Cook.

Murray, Donald. 1996. *Crafting a Life in Essay, Story, and Poem.* Portsmouth, NH: Boynton/Cook.

Romano, Tom. 2000. *Blending Genre, Altering Style.* Portsmouth, NH: Boynton/Cook.

Rule, Rebecca, and Susan Wheeler. 1993. *Creating the Story.* Portsmouth, NH: Heinemann.

Stern, Jerome. 1991. *Making Shapely Fiction.* New York: W. W. Norton.

Wilde, Jack. 1993. *A Door Opens.* Portsmouth, NH: Heinemann.

Appendix

Student Materials for Classroom and At-Home Use

In the Classroom
Peer Response Record
Spelling Check
Scenes as Skits
Story Trip Observations
Weekly Reading Focus
Writing Actions to Show Feelings
Writing Quotations to Show Feelings

At Home
Writing a Scene
Studying Appearance
Studying Actions
Studying Dialogue
Studying Setting

Peer Response Record

Author _____

Working Title _____

Date Started_____Date Set Aside_____Date Published_____

* * * * * * * * * * * * * * *

Date	Respondent	Revision Discussion Checklist
____	_____	1. The <u>lead</u> pulls us into the story.
____	_____	2. The <u>characters</u> try to solve a problem.
____	_____	3. All the <u>events</u> in the story make sense.
____	_____	4. We know where the action takes <u>place</u>.
____	_____	5. We see and hear characters in <u>scenes</u>.
____	_____	6. The <u>ending</u> brings the story to a close.
____	_____	7. The <u>title</u> catches our interest but doesn't give away the story.

Date	Editor	Editing Checklist
____	_____	1. Spelling check completed.
____	_____	2. Punctuation and capitals checked.

Spelling Check

Suspicious Word	Second Guess	Final Spelling
_____	_____	_____
_____	_____	_____
_____	_____	_____
_____	_____	_____
_____	_____	_____
_____	_____	_____
_____	_____	_____
_____	_____	_____
_____	_____	_____
_____	_____	_____
_____	_____	_____
_____	_____	_____
_____	_____	_____
_____	_____	_____
_____	_____	_____
_____	_____	_____
_____	_____	_____
_____	_____	_____
_____	_____	_____
_____	_____	_____
_____	_____	_____
_____	_____	_____
_____	_____	_____

Scenes as Skits

Actor #1 _____   Actor #2 _____

* * * * * * *

Skit Title_____

The Characters

     #1. Name _____ acts like _____

     _____

     #2. Name _____ acts like _____

     _____

The Setting

     Place _____

     Time _____

The Problem

     _____

     _____

Story Trip Observations

Sounds Like   Looks Like

Feels Like   Smells Like

Weekly Reading Focus

Date _____ Book Title _____

Focus Question _____

Response _____

_____

_____

_____

_____

_____

Date _____ Book Title _____

Focus Question _____

Response _____

_____

_____

_____

_____

_____

_____

Writing Actions to Show Feelings

Action	Feelings

1. "Presently he saw another, this one   _____

   quite definitely a fish, calmly drifting

   in the pool. . . . He lunged at it, lost his   _____

   footing, and went down with a splash

   that would scare off any fish for miles   _____

   around."

   —from *Sign of the Beaver*, p. 47.

2. _____   _____

   _____   _____

   _____   _____

3. _____   _____

   _____   _____

   _____   _____

Writing Quotations to Show Feelings

	Quotation	Feelings
1.	"How dare you talk to me like that, young man!"	_____
2.	"Could I please have another chance? I promise I'll never do it again!"	_____
3.	_____ _____ _____	_____
4.	_____ _____ _____	_____
5.	_____ _____ _____	_____

Homework: Writing a Scene

Sit somewhere in your house. Use all your senses to <u>observe</u> what is going on around you.

1. Close your eyes and listen. What do you hear?

2. Sniff the air. What do you smell?

3. Open your eyes and look around. What do you see?

4. Reach out and touch nearby objects. How do they feel?

Write a two-character scene that takes place where you're sitting. Make sure to include dialogue, action, and the information you gathered when you made your sense observations.

Homework: Studying Appearance

Observe the appearance of someone in your family. Look carefully at what this person wears, how he or she combs his or her hair, and other characteristics that makes him or her different from any other person you know.

Words that describe this character's appearance are _____

_____

_____

Write a lead to a story that includes information about this character's appearance.

_____

_____

_____

_____

_____

_____

_____

_____

_____

_____

_____

Homework: Studying Actions

<u>Observe</u> someone doing something at home. Watch what he or she does with his or her hands, face, and body.

<u>Words that describe</u> this character's actions are_____

_____

_____

<u>These actions show</u> that this character is feeling_____

_____

_____

<u>Describe what this character is doing</u> as if it were part of a story.

_____

_____

_____

_____

_____

_____

_____

_____

_____

_____

Homework: Studying Dialogue

Listen to two people talking for a few minutes. Watch what they do with their hands, face, and body. Notice whether they listen to each other, talk over each other, or hesitate before they speak.

Dialogue: What do they <u>say</u>? "Use quotation marks!" _____

_____

_____

_____

_____

_____

_____

_____

What do they <u>do</u> as they speak? _____

_____

_____

What do you think they are <u>feeling</u> during this conversation?

_____

_____

_____

Homework: Studying Setting

Turn off the sound and watch a favorite noncartoon television program for ten minutes. Look carefully at where the action takes place.

<u>List</u> all the settings you see.

_____

_____

_____

_____

_____

_____

_____

_____

References

Atwell, Nancie. 1998. *In the Middle.* Portsmouth, NH: Heinemann.

Bauer, Marion. 1986. *On My Honor.* New York: Dell.

Benchley, Nathaniel. 1987. *Sam the Minuteman.* New York: Harper Trophy.

Black, Sheila. 1994. *Little Giants.* St. Petersburg, FL: Willowisp Press.

Burke, Carol, and Tinsley, Molly Best. 1993. *The Creative Process.* New York: St. Martin's Press.

Burroway, Janet. 2000. *A Guide to Narrative Craft.* 5th ed. New York: Longman.

Calkins, Lucy. 1989. *The Art of Teaching Writing.* Portsmouth, NH: Heinemann.

———. 1991. *Living Between the Lines.* Portsmouth, NH: Heinemann.

Chiarella, Tom. 1998. *Writing Dialogue.* Cincinnati: Story Press.

Collier, James, and Christopher Collier. 1981. *Jump Ship to Freedom.* New York: Dell.

Cushman, Karen. 1995. *The Midwife's Apprentice.* New York: Clarion.

Dyson, Anne Haas. 1997. *Writing Superheroes: Contemporary Childhood, Popular Culture, and Classroom Literacy.* New York: Teachers College Press.

Egan, Kieran. 1988. *Primary Understanding.* New York: Routledge.

Gardiner, James. 1984. *The Art of Fiction.* New York: Alfred A. Knopf.

Graves, Donald. 1989. *Experiments with Fiction.* Portsmouth, NH: Heinemann.

———. 1994. *A Fresh Look at Writing.* Portsmouth, NH: Heinemann.

Harste, Jerome, Kathy Short, and Carolyn Burke. 1988. *Creating Classrooms for Authors.* Portsmouth, NH: Heinemann.

Jason, Philip K., and Allan Lefcowitz. 1990. *Creative Writer's Handbook.* Englewood Cliffs, NJ: Prentice-Hall.

Leland, Christopher T. 1998. *The Art of Compelling Fiction.* Cincinnati: Story Press.

L'Engle, Madeleine. 1962. *A Wrinkle in Time.* New York: Dell.

Lutwach, Leonard. 1984. *The Role of Place in Literature.* New York: Syracuse University Press.

Mullins, Lisa, ed. 1987. *The Evolution of Colonial Architecture.* Pittstown, NJ: The National Historical Society, Main Street Press.

Newkirk, Thomas, March 2000, "Misreading Masculinity: Speculations on the Great Gender Gap in Writing," *Language Arts*, Vol. 77, No. 4.

Paterson, Katherine. 1972. *Bridge to Terabithia.* New York: Ricky Crowell.

Rule, Rebecca, and Susan Wheeler. 1993. *Creating the Story.* Portsmouth, NH: Heinemann.

Speare, Elizabeth George. 1983. *Sign of the Beaver.* New York: Dell.

Stern, Jerome. 1991. *Making Shapely Fiction.* New York: W. W. Norton.

Stine, R. L. 1995. *Horror at Camp Jellyjam.* New York: Scholastic Paperbacks.

———. 1996. *Ghost Camp.* New York: Apple.

———. 1998. *Fright Camp.* New York: Demco Media.

White, Ruth. 1996. *Bell Prater's Boy.* New York: Dell.